CHOSEN and LOVED

Healing for the Hurting, Rejected, and Overlooked

CLINT BYARS

Chosen By God: A Heart Journey of Identity, Love, and Transformation

© 2025 Clint Byars

All rights reserved.

No part of this publication may be reproduced, stored in a retrieval system, or transmitted in any form or by any means—electronic, mechanical, photocopying, recording, or otherwise—without the prior written permission of the publisher, except in the case of brief quotations embodied in critical articles or reviews.

All scripture quotations, unless otherwise indicated, are taken from the New King James Version®. Copyright © 1982 by Thomas Nelson. Used by permission. All rights reserved.

Some additional scripture quotations are taken from the New American Standard Bible® (NASB), © The Lockman Foundation 1960, 1962, 1963, 1968, 1971, 1972, 1973, 1975, 1977, 1995, 2020. Used by permission.

Also referenced: English Standard Version (ESV) and Amplified Bible (AMP), used by permission where noted.

ISBN: 979-8-9913215-2-5

First Edition: 2025

For more information, visit:

www.clintbyars.com or www.forward.church

TABLE OF CONTENTS

Introduction 5
You Were Always Wanted 5

Part 1: You Were Chosen—Before Time Began 9
Chapter 1: The Treasure in the Field 12
Chapter 2: Loved First, Chosen Forever 17
Chapter 3: Understanding Rejection and Why It Hurts
So Deeply 23

Part 2: What Do You Believe About God? 31
Chapter 4: Healing Your Image of God 34
Chapter 5: Created for Intimacy with a Good Father 44
Chapter 6: What Do You Believe About Yourself? 52

**PART 3: The Word in the HeartHealing From the
Inside Out** 65
Chapter 7: Letting the Word Discern Your Heart 68
Chapter 8: Bringing the Lie to the Cross 77
Chapter 9: Putting On the New Man 88

Part 4: Letting the Word Reveal the Heart 99
Chapter 10: The Word Discerns What You Believe 102
Chapter 11: From Exposure to Healing 111

Part 5: Walking with God Through Renewal .. 119
Chapter 12: Ephesians **4:22–24** in Practice 122
Chapter 13: Example Walkthroughs 131

Part 6: Intimacy with God When You've Been Hurt **140**

Chapter 14: God Is Safe But Pain Makes Him Feel Far 143

Chapter 15: Learning to Receive Love Again............................152

Part 7: Living with a Renewed Heart **160**

Chapter 16: Daily Rhythms of Heart Transformation............163

Chapter 17: Staying Rooted in Grace 171

Chapter 18: Transformation That Lasts.....................................178

Conclusion: 184

About the Author 187

INTRODUCTION
YOU WERE ALWAYS WANTED

Before you were ever born, you were known. Before you ever called out to God, He had already set His love on you. You are not random. You are not forgotten. You are not a mistake. You are chosen.

Many of us carry silent questions deep in our hearts: *Why wasn't I picked? Why did they leave? Why wasn't I enough?* Whether it was a parent who abandoned you, a friend who rejected you, a relationship that broke your heart, or a community that excluded you—you've felt the sting. Rejection marks the soul and quietly suggests that something is wrong with you. But that's not how God sees you.

In fact, your story begins long before the pain. According to Jesus, **you are the treasure hidden in the field**—so valuable to the Father that He gave everything to purchase the whole world just to have you (Matthew 13:44). You are the joy that was set before Jesus, the reason He endured the cross and resisted every temptation of sin and shame (Hebrews 12:2). God has never been indifferent toward you. He is a Father at heart, and His desire has always been to bring you home—not as a servant trying to earn love, but as a **child receiving it freely.**

But here's where it gets complex. Life doesn't always look like love. We live in a broken world, and when rejection or abuse enters the picture, it's easy to wonder, Where was God? Maybe you've even judged Him in your heart—seen Him as distant, cold, silent… maybe even cruel.

If you've ever thought, If God really loved me, He wouldn't have let that happen, you're not alone. But that view assumes God is micromanaging life's pain, when in fact, **He gave mankind dominion of the earth** (Genesis 1:26–28). In love, He gave us free will—and that freedom has led to unspeakable pain at the hands of others. **God does not control people,** and He does not author evil. He doesn't need the abuse, betrayal, or trauma in your story to teach you a lesson. His heart is always to heal, restore, and redeem. But He won't force His love. He is a gentleman—but make no mistake, **He absolutely wants you.**

You were not created to be a servant groveling for scraps. You were created to be a son or daughter, fully restored and alive in love. Like the father in the story of the prodigal son, God doesn't even let you finish your shame-filled speech. He covers you in robes of righteousness and calls you His own.

This book is a journey of the heart. It's about trading rejection for belonging, shame for righteousness, confusion for clarity, and fear for love. It's about planting God's Word in your heart, letting it reveal what you truly believe, and allowing the Holy Spirit to guide you in putting off lies and putting on truth. It's about intimacy with a God who is not like the ones who hurt you. A God who proved His love through the cross.

This book will give you tools, exercises, and daily rhythms to help you renew your mind and heart, **don't become dogmatic.** These tools are here to serve your healing, not control your process. If one practice or exercise resonates deeply with you, lean into it. If another feels heavy or unhelpful in a certain season, let it go without guilt. The Holy Spirit is your guide. Grace will lead you.

You don't have to stay stuck. You don't have to earn healing. You only need to say "yes" to the truth.

You are chosen. You are not alone. And your healing begins now.

PART 1:
YOU WERE CHOSEN— BEFORE TIME BEGAN

CHOSEN AND LOVED

God didn't start loving you when you got it together. He loved you before you were born.

Before you ever had a name, a wound, or a failure, **you were chosen.** Before your first breath, before your first heartbreak, even before the world was formed—God saw you, knew you, and wanted you. This is not poetic language; this is the unshakable truth at the core of the gospel.

You are not the result of random biology or a cosmic accident. You are not just "tolerated" by God. You are **wanted,** deeply and eternally. You are the treasure hidden in the field that Jesus spoke about—a treasure so precious that the Father gave everything to buy the field just to have you (Matthew 13:44).

But most of us don't feel chosen. We feel passed over. Unseen. Rejected.

Maybe it was a parent who failed to nurture you, a sibling who shamed you, a friend group that excluded you, or a relationship that ended with no explanation. Maybe it was a job that said no, a church that pushed you away, or a society that made you feel like you didn't fit in. Or maybe, at the deepest level, you've felt rejected by God Himself—like He abandoned you in your darkest moments.

These experiences leave an imprint. Rejection isn't just painful—it's **formational.** It tries to define your identity. And unless it's confronted with a greater truth, it will speak louder than the voice of God in your heart.

That's why we're starting here.

Before we can talk about renewing your mind, healing your emotions, or transforming your habits, we have to go all the way back to the beginning—to the **eternal decision** God made about you: **You are chosen. You are loved. And you are worth everything to Him.**

In this part of the journey, you'll confront the lies of rejection and meet the God who never stopped wanting you. You'll let the truth of your chosenness settle into your heart and become the foundation for everything that follows. Because until you know you're wanted, it's hard to receive anything else from Him.

Let's begin here—with the love that started before time.

CHAPTER 1:
THE TREASURE IN THE FIELD

You are worth everything to God.

"The kingdom of heaven is like treasure hidden in a field, which a man found and hid; and for joy over it he goes and sells all that he has and buys that field."
—Matthew 13:44

Jesus used parables to help us see the unseen. In Matthew 13:44, He reveals a glimpse of the Father's heart. He tells of a man who discovers a hidden treasure in a field. Once he finds it, he hides it again—because he doesn't want to lose it. Then, overflowing with joy, he sells **everything** to buy the entire field just to get that one treasure.

You are that treasure.

And the one who gave everything to have you is Jesus.

This is not just a nice metaphor—it's a declaration of your value to God. You may not feel like treasure. Life may have covered you in dirt and lies, buried you in fear or rejection. But God saw beyond it all. He saw what others overlooked. He saw you. And He didn't hesitate— He paid for the entire world with the blood of His Son to redeem what He desired most: **your heart.**

God Didn't Wait for You to Prove Your Worth

It's natural to measure our value by performance. Did we succeed? Did we meet the standard? Did someone choose us?

But God didn't wait for you to be perfect. He didn't choose you because of your good behavior, strong faith, or spiritual track record. He chose you **because He loved you.** That's it. That's the whole reason.

> *"But God demonstrates His own love toward us, in that while we were still sinners, Christ died for us."*
> —Romans 5:8

While we were still broken, Jesus paid the highest price. And He didn't do it reluctantly. Matthew 13 says the man **"for joy"** sold everything to get the treasure. That's how Jesus felt about you. **You were the joy set before Him.**

> *"For the joy that was set before Him, He endured the cross…"*
> —Hebrews 12:2

The cross was not just about defeating sin and death—it was about removing everything that stood in the way of relationship with you. Jesus didn't die to convince God to love you. He died **because** God already did.

The Treasure Was Always There—Even When You Didn't See It

You may not feel like treasure. Maybe you feel buried. Forgotten. Covered by shame or failure. But buried treasure doesn't lose its value just because it's hidden.

God never stopped seeing your worth.

He never lost sight of your design. You were created in His image (Genesis 1:27). He knit you together with purpose and delight (Psalm 139:13–16). And even when life, sin, or rejection tried to bury that truth, He already had a plan to redeem it.

You don't become valuable once you clean yourself up.

CHOSEN AND LOVED

You are valuable because **God made you,** God knows you, and God wants you.

Reflection

* What lies have tried to bury your worth?

* Can you picture Jesus finding you like the man in the parable—recognizing your value, rejoicing, and giving all to redeem you?

* What would change in your heart if you truly believed you are God's treasure?

Confession

"I am God's treasure.

He saw my worth and gave everything to redeem me.

I am not forgotten, overlooked, or unwanted.

I am chosen, valued, and deeply loved."

> **Prayer**
>
> Father, I've spent so long believing I was too broken to be wanted. But You saw treasure where I saw dirt. Thank You for paying the highest price to have me. I receive Your love, not based on what I've done, but on who You are. Let this truth take root in my heart. Help me to believe I am valuable, not someday—**now**. Let the love that moved You to the cross define me. I am Yours.

CHAPTER 2
LOVED FIRST, CHOSEN FOREVER

> *God's love is not a reaction—it's the origin of everything.*

"We love Him because He first loved us."
—1 John 4:19

We often imagine that our relationship with God began when we decided to love Him. But scripture tells a very different story: **our love is a response.** The truth is, God's love was already moving toward you long before you ever turned your attention toward Him. Your love is a reflection of His. Your seeking is only possible because He was already drawing you.

You were **loved first.**

That might sound simple, but it cuts to the root of so many spiritual and emotional struggles. We struggle to trust God because deep down, we wonder if He really likes us. We try to please Him because we fear rejection. We serve, strive, and sacrifice—not from joy, but from insecurity. Why? Because we haven't fully believed the first truth: I am already loved.

When love is something you work for, it becomes fragile. You're always one mistake away from feeling disqualified. But when love is the **starting point**, everything changes. You can rest. You can heal. You can begin to love others freely, because you're not trying to earn your place anymore—you know you're secure.

You Were Chosen Before You Were Born

> *"He chose us in Him before the foundation of the world, that we should be holy and without blame before Him in love."*
> —Ephesians 1:4

God's love for you didn't start at the cross—it was revealed at the cross. It started **before time began.** He saw you. He knew you. He wanted you. Not a future version of you, but you as you are.

This matters deeply, because many believers assume God only loves the version of them that has it all together. The "in-Christ" version. The one who prays more, sins less, forgives quickly, and always does the right thing. But if God only loved the cleaned-up version of you, then His love would be based on your performance. It would fluctuate.

But His love never fluctuates.

Romans 5:8 says that "while we were still sinners, Christ died for us." That means your mess didn't scare Him away—it moved Him toward you. He didn't wait for you to repent before loving you. He loved you **into repentance.** His kindness is what leads you to change (Romans 2:4).

Love Is the Foundation for Believing

This is why so many people struggle to walk in faith. Faith doesn't work when the heart is uncertain of love. The heart was created to believe in the context of security. You can't fully trust someone you fear might reject you. That's why 1 John 4:18 says that *perfect love casts out fear.*

Fear and faith do not grow in the same soil. And when the heart is saturated in rejection, it's hard to receive truth, even when you hear it.

This is why believing the gospel must begin with this reality: **God loved you first.**

He didn't send Jesus to change His mind about you. He sent Jesus to reveal what He already felt.

You Were Not Just Saved—You Were Adopted

"Having predestined us to adoption as sons by Jesus Christ to Himself, according to the good pleasure of His will."
—Ephesians 1:5

Salvation isn't just about escaping hell or being forgiven—it's about being brought into God's family. You weren't just rescued. You were **adopted.** He wanted you to belong. He wanted you to carry His name.

This is so important because many believers live with a servant mindset: grateful to be in the house, but afraid to sit at the table. But you're not a servant. You're a son. You're a daughter. And God loves you with the same love He has for Jesus (John 17:23).

He isn't tolerating you. He delights in you. And when you begin to believe that, everything in your inner world starts to change.

What If You Really Believed This?

Take a moment and ask yourself:

* What would change in my heart if I truly believed God loved me first and not because of any performance on my part?
* Would I still strive so hard to prove myself?
* Would I still carry shame over the past?
* Would I still fear being left out, overlooked, or rejected?

You were never on trial. You were never competing for God's attention. The verdict is in: **You are loved. You are chosen. You are His.**

This is the soil where true transformation grows. This is the foundation for healing, faith, and identity. This is where your new life begins—with love.

Reflection

* What have you believed about why God loves you?
* Are you still trying to earn His acceptance?
* What would it look like to rest in His love today?

Confession

"God loved me first.

He chose me before I was born.

His love is not fragile or earned—it is eternal and secure.

I don't have to strive for His affection.

I am His beloved child, adopted and accepted forever."

> **Prayer**
> Father, thank You for loving me before I ever knew You. Thank You for choosing me, not based on my worth or performance, but because You are love. Help me to receive that love, fully and freely. Heal every place in my heart that still strives for what You've already given. Let me live from love, not for love. Let Your love define me, anchor me, and transform me. I believe You loved me first—and that changes everything.
> Amen.

CHAPTER 3:
UNDERSTANDING REJECTION AND WHY IT HURTS SO DEEPLY

> *Rejection doesn't just hurt—it tries to define you.*

Rejection is one of the most painful experiences a human heart can endure. Whether it came from a parent, a sibling, a friend, a boyfriend or girlfriend, a job interview, a school application, or even a church—rejection leaves a wound. And over time, that wound can begin to speak.

It says: *You're not wanted.*

It whispers: *You're not enough.*

It assumes: *You'll be rejected again.*

These messages take root in the heart if they're not confronted by truth. If we don't know we are loved, chosen, and accepted by God, we will subconsciously carry the identity that rejection handed us.

The Many Faces of Rejection

Rejection isn't always loud. Sometimes it's subtle. Sometimes it's not what was said, but what was never said.

* A parent who withheld affection or made love feel conditional.

* A sibling who constantly compared you or made you feel inferior.

* Classmates who excluded you or mocked you.

* A relationship that ended without explanation.

* A job that didn't call you back.

* A church that judged you for being honest about your struggle.

* A society that made you feel invisible.

* Or maybe the hardest one of all: the feeling that God Himself rejected you.

Rejection has layers. It hits differently depending on the source. Rejection by someone you barely know stings. Rejection by someone you love cuts to the bone.

Why It Hurts So Much

We were created for connection. Genesis tells us we were made in the image of a relational God. From the very beginning, we were designed to be known, loved, and accepted. That's why rejection feels so unnatural. It violates the way we were made.

The pain of rejection doesn't mean you're weak. It means you're human.

Modern psychological studies confirm this. Research using fMRI brain scans has shown that social rejection activates the same areas of the brain as physical pain. When you are rejected, your brain processes it like an injury. It also affects your body's hormonal systems: cortisol (the stress hormone) rises, oxytocin (the bonding hormone) drops, and the amygdala (your threat detector) goes on high alert. Your body interprets rejection as danger, and over time, that stress can become chronic.

But here's the deeper issue: rejection doesn't just hurt; it shapes how we see ourselves if we don't confront it. It forms beliefs. It programs emotional patterns. It trains us to expect more of the same.

This is where we encounter the spiritual and emotional condition of being vexed.

What Does It Mean to Be Vexed?

To be vexed means that something happened to you, and it settled deep in your soul. It agitated your emotions, created internal conflict, and over time, it began to **write on your heart.**

Sometimes we swear we won't repeat the pattern. We vow to never be like the ones who hurt us. But because information plus emotion creates belief, that painful event becomes a core message in our subconscious. And even if it's irrational, if the belief stays unhealed, we often live it out.

If we were victimized, abused, betrayed, or repeatedly rejected, that trauma becomes a lens. Without realizing it, we filter the world through that lens. And worse, we begin to believe something false about **ourselves.**

* *"I'm not good enough."*

* *"I'm hard to love."*

* *"I always mess things up."*

* *"People always leave."*

* *"God must not care."*

We live out of the beliefs of our hearts, especially the ones we believe about ourselves. And unless those beliefs are rewritten, we will repeat the very cycle we swore to break.

But here's the hope: **this book will show you how to rewrite those beliefs.**

God doesn't want you living from the script rejection handed you. He wants to write new truth on your heart—truth rooted in His Word and His love. He wants to show you **His true heart for you.** Through Scripture, reflection, prayer, and practical steps, I will help you plant the truth of God's acceptance so deeply that it displaces the pain of rejection.

You can be healed. You can be free. And it starts by believing that rejection is not your identity.

When Rejection Makes You Question God

For many people, the deepest layer of rejection is

spiritual. You may have wondered, *If God really loved me, why did He let that happen?* If He saw me, why didn't He stop it? If He's good, why didn't He intervene?

These are not rebellious questions. These are honest cries from the human heart.

But here is the truth: God did not author your rejection. He did not orchestrate your abuse, neglect, or betrayal. He never partners with sin to teach you a lesson. He never uses cruelty to shape your character.

God is not controlling every circumstance. He gave mankind dominion over the earth (Genesis 1:26). That means humans have the power to choose—and tragically, people often use that power to hurt one another. But that does not mean God is passive. He is redemptive. He enters into our pain. And in Jesus, He provided the ultimate healing for rejection: **total, eternal acceptance.**

God Is Not Like the Ones Who Hurt You

One of the most important revelations you can have is this: **God is not like the people who rejected you.**

He is not emotionally distant like your dad.

He is not conditional like your ex.

He is not silent like the people who ignored your pain.

He is a Father. He is love. He is near to the brokenhearted.

> *"Though my father and mother forsake me, the Lord will receive me."*
> —Psalm 27:10

In Jesus, God opened His arms and said, "You are welcome here. You are mine."

You are not a burden. You are not too much. You are not invisible.

You are chosen.

You are accepted.

You are loved.

Reflection

* Who rejected you that you still carry pain from?

* Have you assumed God is like that person?

* What would change in you if you believed God fully accepts you?

Confession

"God has not rejected me.

People may have hurt me, ignored me, or abandoned me—but He never will.

I am not defined by rejection.

I am defined by His love.

I am fully accepted in the Beloved."

> **Prayer**
> Father, You know every wound I carry. You know who walked away, who didn't see me, who made me feel small. But You are not like them. You are faithful. You are present. And You never turn me away. Help me to let go of the lies rejection planted in me. Heal every scar with Your truth. Speak to the places in me that still wonder if I'm wanted. And let Your acceptance be louder than every voice that ever said I wasn't enough.
> Amen.

PART 2
WHAT DO YOU BELIEVE ABOUT GOD?

CHOSEN AND LOVED

Your healing depends on the image of God you carry in your heart.

We've all formed an idea of what God is like. Whether from church, childhood, culture, or crisis, we carry around internal pictures of Him—some accurate, many distorted. And those images shape everything: how we pray, how we trust, how we receive, and whether we even want to be close to Him at all.

For some, God is a distant observer—watching but uninvolved. For others, He's a strict judge, easily disappointed and slow to forgive. Some see Him as a cosmic puppeteer, micromanaging suffering "for a reason," and therefore emotionally untrustworthy. And tragically, many carry into their view of God the traits of the very people who hurt them.

If your earthly father was angry or absent, it's easy to assume God is too.

If people used religion to control or reject you, you may believe God's love is just as conditional.

But here's the truth: **Jesus is the perfect image of the Father.** And He came to show us what God is really like—kind, compassionate, forgiving, full of grace and truth. When you've seen Him, you've seen the Father

(John 14:9).

This section of your journey is crucial, because you cannot rest in the love of a God you don't trust. You cannot be transformed by truth if you secretly believe God is the source of your pain. Until you let Him reveal His true heart, your heart will stay guarded.

But here's the good news: you don't have to guess what God is like. You can look at Jesus—His words, His actions, His sacrifice—and know beyond doubt: **God is good, and God wants you.**

In the next chapters, we'll confront the lies many people believe about God and replace them with the truth of who He is. You'll discover that He is not the one who abandoned you, hurt you, or confused you. He is the One who came to rescue and restore you.

Let the healing begin with this one powerful shift: seeing the Father through the eyes of Jesus.

CHAPTER 4:
HEALING YOUR IMAGE OF GOD

> *You can't trust a God you secretly believe is against you.*

Everyone has an image of God—not just a doctrinal one, but an emotional one. It's the God you picture in your heart when you're afraid, when you've failed, or when you suffer loss. For many, that inner picture is blurry, harsh, or even terrifying. And it shows up in subtle ways:

* You brace for disappointment when you pray.

* You expect punishment when things go wrong.

* You question His goodness when life hurts.

* You wonder if He's withholding from you or testing you.

We often say God is love, but inwardly we wonder: Is He really? Especially when pain is personal.

This is why healing your image of God is so vital. You cannot receive love from someone you fear. You cannot trust someone you think is against you. If your view of God is shaped by trauma, religion, or painful experiences, then everything else in your faith will be affected. But the good news is this: **you can rebuild your image of God on the foundation of truth.**

To begin that healing, there are three essential areas we must explore to understand the true character of God.

1. Who God Says He Is

When God takes the time in Scripture to describe Himself, we should pause and take it seriously. He is not hiding His nature—He is declaring it. The names of God throughout the Bible are not just titles; they are invitations to trust.

* *Jehovah Rapha* – The Lord who heals you (Exodus 15:26)

* *Jehovah Jireh* – The Lord who provides (Genesis 22:14)

* *Jehovah Shalom* – The Lord your peace (Judges 6:24)

* *Jehovah Nissi* – The Lord your banner of victory (Exodus 17:15)

* *Jehovah Tsidkenu* – The Lord your righteousness (Jeremiah 23:6)

* *Jehovah Rohi* – The Lord your shepherd (Psalm 23:1)

When He calls Himself your Shepherd, He is promising to guide you, feed you, protect you, and restore your soul. When He says He is your Healer, He's not just talking about physical illness—He's speaking to your broken heart, your wounded memories, and your emotional scars.

God has revealed Himself with intention. These names are not metaphors—they are realities. And they give us permission to expect Him to be who He says He is.

There's no greater source for understanding God than when He tells you directly who He is. And His declarations are consistent with His actions throughout

Scripture.

2. Who Jesus Shows the Father To Be

The clearest picture we have of God is Jesus. Hebrews 1:3 says Jesus is "the exact representation of His being." Colossians 1:15 calls Him "the image of the invisible God." When Jesus walked the earth, He didn't just show us what a godly man looks like—He showed us **what God looks like.**

* And what did He do?

* He healed the sick.

* He raised the dead.

* He forgave sinners.

* He had compassion on the broken.

* He restored the shamed.

* He welcomed the outcasts.

* He silenced storms.

* He set captives free.

He did not ignore sin, but He also never used guilt to manipulate people. He never partnered with fear to provoke repentance. His kindness led people to turn back to God.

And when it comes to God's judgment and wrath, Jesus didn't sidestep it—He absorbed it.

On the cross, we see the justice of God poured out on sin—not on you, but on Jesus. As 2 Corinthians 5:21 says, "God made Him who knew no sin to be sin for us, that we might become the righteousness of God in Him."

God was not ignoring sin; He was destroying its power. That is what the wrath of God looks like: it was fully satisfied in Christ. This doesn't mean sin doesn't matter—it means Jesus paid for it so you don't have to.

Because of that, you now stand before God **as you should be**—righteous, clean, and whole.

Righteousness means: you are as you should be before God.

You didn't earn it. You received it by grace through faith. Grace is not just undeserved favor; grace is the very power of God working in your heart to transform you. When you need help, God doesn't expect you to fake it. He invites you to come boldly to His throne of grace, where you will receive **mercy when you've missed** it and grace when you need strength to overcome (Hebrews 4:16).

Jesus came not only to reveal the Father's heart but to make you right with Him forever. That is the gospel.

Jesus showed us a God who is emotionally available. A Father who welcomes questions. A Shepherd who pursues. A Redeemer who sees every wound. Through Jesus, we see that God is not cold, harsh, or detached—He's moved by compassion.

3. What Jesus Accomplished at the Cross

Everything you need to know about the goodness of God can be seen at the cross. In one act of love, Jesus bore your pain, carried your shame, defeated sin, conquered death, and opened the way for full reconciliation with the Father.

Isaiah 53 says:

* He was pierced for your transgressions.

* He was crushed for your iniquities.

* The punishment that brought you peace was upon Him.

* By His wounds, you are healed.

Other scriptures reveal that through the cross, you received:

* Forgiveness of sins (Colossians 1:14)

* Justification—declared righteous before God (Romans 5:1)

* Reconciliation—brought back into relationship (2 Corinthians 5:18)

* Cleansing of your conscience (Hebrews 9:14)

* Freedom from condemnation (Romans 8:1)

* Victory over the powers of darkness (Colossians 2:15)

* Bold access to God's presence (Hebrews 10:19–22)

The cross is the proof that God is not your accuser. He is your rescuer. He is not holding your sins against you— He placed them on Jesus. He's not waiting for you to earn your place—He gave it to you as a gift.

And if the cross tells us anything, it is this: **God would rather die than be separated from you.**

The more you meditate on the cross, the more your heart begins to see clearly again. Love becomes believable. Grace becomes real. You begin to recognize that God is for you, not against you.

The Prodigal Son: A Better Picture of the Father

In Luke 15, Jesus tells a story that shifts everything. A son rebels, wastes everything, and decides to return home—not as a son, but as a servant. He rehearses a speech of shame, assuming he must earn back his place.

But the father runs. He doesn't let the son grovel. He interrupts the speech, embraces him, clothes him, and throws a feast.

That's how God responds to you.

He's not interested in your self-punishment. He's not holding your past over your head. He's not a Father who shames or withholds. He's a Father who rejoices the moment you turn your heart toward Him.

You are not merely tolerated in His presence. You are **celebrated.**

Healing Begins With Seeing Clearly

Transformation doesn't begin with doing more or trying harder. It begins with seeing God as He truly is.

> *"They looked to Him and were radiant, and their faces were not ashamed."*

—Psalm 34:5

When you see Him clearly, shame melts. Fear fades. You stop flinching when you pray. You stop wondering if He's mad at you. You start to believe again.

And that changes everything.

Reflection

* How do you picture God when you're afraid or ashamed?
* Where did that image come from?
* Does it match the heart of Jesus and the truth of the cross?

Confession

"God is not the one who hurt me.

He is not distant, silent, or angry.

He is exactly like Jesus.

Compassionate, present, and full of grace.

He calls Himself my healer, my shepherd, and my peace.

I trust His heart. I trust His love."

Prayer

Father, I repent for believing lies about You. Not just theological ones, but emotional ones. I thought You were distant. I thought You were punishing me. But now I see the truth: You are like Jesus. You heal. You restore. You forgive. You run to me, not from me. Let every distorted image fall away. Let me see Your heart with clarity and confidence. Let Your goodness rebuild my trust.

Amen.

CHOSEN AND LOVED

CHAPTER 5:
CREATED FOR INTIMACY WITH A GOOD FATHER

You were made for connection, not performance.

God didn't create you for religious duty—He created you for relationship. Not a distant, formal kind of relationship, but real, heart-level intimacy. Before the fall, Adam and Eve walked with God in the cool of the day. That's what was lost—and that's what Jesus came to restore.

But let's be honest: intimacy with God can feel difficult,

especially when you've been hurt.

When human relationships have been marked by betrayal, abandonment, rejection, or abuse, it becomes hard to trust—even with God. You may believe He loves you, but struggle to feel close to Him. You may know He's good in theory, but feel unsure whether He's safe with your heart.

This is especially true when you've been rejected. Rejection writes something deep into our emotional memory. A painful social rejection—especially by a parent, partner, or spiritual leader—can actually activate the same areas of the brain as physical pain. Studies have shown that the experience of rejection increases activity in the anterior cingulate cortex and the insula, parts of the brain associated with pain processing. It also alters cortisol levels, the stress hormone, which can linger long after the experience is over.

In other words, rejection doesn't just break your heart—it changes your brain.

And if you've ever been rejected by people who claimed to represent God, the wound cuts even deeper.

What It Means to Be Vexed

There's a biblical word for the emotional aftermath of hurt that continues to shape how we live: vexed.

To be vexed is to be distressed, wounded, or burdened in soul—especially from something that was done to you. Often it's something you swore you'd never repeat, yet it keeps showing up. Why? Because information plus emotion writes beliefs on the heart.

When you're hurt—especially as a child or in a moment of vulnerability—the combination of what happened and what you felt creates an imprint. That imprint becomes a belief. And you live from the beliefs of your heart—especially the ones you believe about yourself.

If you were told or shown that you were unwanted, unworthy, or defective, it may not matter how many sermons you hear. Until your heart is healed and reprogrammed, you will struggle to believe differently.

This is why we must renew the heart, not just the mind. The mind understands logic, but the heart understands love.

The Father's Response to Rejection

God does not minimize your pain. He doesn't brush

off your rejection or expect you to simply "get over it." Instead, He steps into your pain through Jesus—and takes it on Himself.

Isaiah 53:3 says Jesus was "despised and rejected by men, a man of sorrows and acquainted with grief." He not only understands your rejection—He felt it in the deepest ways:

* Betrayed by a friend
* Abandoned by His disciples
* Accused by religious leaders
* Mocked by society
* Forsaken on the cross

And He took all of it, so you wouldn't have to live under the weight of it anymore.

At the cross, Jesus absorbed the sting of every rejection. He bore the shame, the sorrow, and the emotional anguish. And now He offers you a new name, a new identity, and a new family.

"Though my father and mother forsake me, the Lord will receive me." – Psalm 27:10

He receives you. He sees you. He delights in you.

Intimacy Is the Goal

God didn't save you just so you could serve Him—He saved you so you could walk with Him. He wants to talk to you, comfort you, laugh with you, guide you. He wants you to feel seen, heard, and valued.

He is not withholding affection. He is not emotionally unavailable. He is not like the people who hurt you.

He is gentle, lowly in heart, and full of compassion. And He has made a way for you to come close:

"Let us then approach God's throne of grace with confidence…" – Hebrews 4:16

The blood of Jesus didn't just forgive your sins—it opened the door to constant fellowship.

How to Begin Healing Through Intimacy

1. Acknowledge the wound.

Begin by admitting what's really in your heart. Tell God the truth—if you've been afraid of Him, angry, or unsure of His love, say it. Honesty is the beginning of intimacy. David, a man after God's heart, poured out his complaints in the Psalms (see Psalm 62:8). God isn't offended by your vulnerability—He's drawn to it.

2. Look to the cross.

The cross is the clearest expression of God's love and His desire for you. When you're unsure of His heart, look again at Jesus—wounded, suffering, rejected in your place. Isaiah 53 says He bore our griefs and carried our sorrows. When you meditate on this, you bring your pain to the very place it was carried. Transformation begins by beholding (2 Corinthians 3:18).

3. Invite Him close.

Intimacy doesn't start with perfect emotions—it starts with invitation. You can say, "God, I don't know how to trust You, but I want to learn." That's enough. In James 4:8, God promises: "Draw near to God, and He will draw near to you." This is a divine law of love—your nearness invites His.

4. Picture Him as He really is.

Use the life of Jesus to paint a new picture of God in your imagination. See Him welcoming the prodigal, healing the leper, protecting the woman caught in adultery. Let the Word reshape your inner image of God. Imagine Him smiling at you, embracing you, singing over you (Zephaniah 3:17). This is not fantasy—it's faith-fueled renewal.

5. Receive, don't strive.

You don't earn closeness—you receive it. John 1:12 says, "To all who received Him…He gave the right to become children of God." Children don't perform for love; they rest in it. Practice letting God love you. Sit in His presence. Let His Word speak louder than your feelings. Don't push to feel something—just be open to Him.

Reflection

* Do I believe God is safe to be close to?

* Where have I experienced rejection that might still influence how I relate to Him?

* What would intimacy with God look like for me, if I believed He truly delighted in me?

Confession

"God, You are not like the ones who hurt me.

You are gentle and kind. You're not pushing me away—you're drawing me close.

I was made to walk with You. And I say yes to that again."

CHOSEN AND LOVED

> **Prayer**
>
> Father, I've felt distant. Maybe I've been afraid of intimacy because of past wounds. But I see now—You're not like them. You're not cold or rejecting. You're full of mercy. Thank You for taking my rejection on the cross. Thank You for making space for me in Your family. I open my heart. Help me learn how to walk closely with You, without fear. I want to know You deeply, and be known by You fully.
>
> Amen.

CHAPTER 6:
WHAT DO YOU BELIEVE ABOUT YOURSELF

Your life follows the direction of your heart's beliefs.

Every decision, every relationship, every pattern you repeat—it all flows from one place: what you believe in your heart.

Proverbs 4:23 says, *"Above all else, guard your heart, for everything you do flows from it."*

And Proverbs 23:7 reminds us, *"As a man thinks in his heart, so is he."*

This isn't just about surface thoughts. It's about deep, emotional heart-level beliefs—what you really think about yourself when no one else is around. Those beliefs may have been shaped by parents, teachers, trauma, culture, or even church experiences. But whether spoken or implied, they have a voice.

* *"You're not enough."*
* *"You're too much."*
* *"You're unlovable."*
* *"You'll never change."*

These are not just thoughts—they're internal scripts. And they run in the background of your life, influencing how you show up, how you relate to God, and what you expect from others.

What Is the Heart?

The heart, in Scripture, is the inner core of your being. It's where your emotions, identity, and beliefs reside. It's deeper than the mind. It's the place where soul and spirit meet, and where God's Spirit touches your life. The heart feels, believes, imagines, and holds onto truth—or lies.

But here's the transformative truth: when you were born again, you were given a new heart.

Ezekiel 36:26 prophesied it: *"I will give you a new heart and put a new spirit in you; I will remove from you your heart of stone and give you a heart of flesh."*

This is the promise of the New Covenant. You no longer have a wicked and deceitful heart. That was the old you, before Christ. Now, you have a heart after God's own heart—a heart that knows His voice and understands His ways.

Hebrews 8:10 confirms: *"I will put my laws in their minds and write them on their hearts. I will be their God, and they will be my people."*

God's righteousness and holiness are now part of your spiritual DNA. Your new heart is not trying to get close to God—it is already united with Him.

Colossians 2:11 adds more clarity: *"In Him you were also circumcised with a circumcision not performed by human hands. Your whole self ruled by the flesh was put off when you were circumcised by Christ."* The Greek word for flesh here is sarx, referring to your old sinful nature, your former humanity apart from God.

God cut that away.

You are no longer hardwired for sin. You are now wired for righteousness, holiness, and love.

When Trauma Writes Over the Truth

So why does it still feel like we're broken sometimes?

Because old beliefs—especially those forged in trauma, abuse, or rejection—can write over the truth of our new heart. They form a false self-image, like a distorted portrait painted over something beautiful. The canvas underneath is pure, but the paint on top tells another story.

These beliefs, rooted in fear or shame, can seem to drive uncontrollable behaviors. That's why even with a new heart, you still need to renew your mind. And because social rejection activates the same brain regions as physical pain, rejection literally hurts—and that pain can shape how we see ourselves, often more than the rejection itself.

If those moments were repeated or intense, they may have formed deeply emotional beliefs in your heart. These beliefs influence your expectations, your choices, and your identity until they are addressed and replaced.

Trauma is more than just something that happened—it's what happened inside of you as a result. And when emotional intensity is paired with meaning, it forms deep beliefs. These beliefs can feel permanent, but they are not. The Word of God is sharper than any two-edged sword and can separate truth from lie, spirit from soul, and reveal what's really there so that healing can begin.

Ephesians 4:22–24 tells us how: *"Put off your old self, which is being corrupted by its deceitful desires... be made new in the attitude of your minds... and put on the new self, created to be like God in true righteousness and holiness."*

You are not trying to become righteous. You already are in spirit. Now you're learning to live from that truth.

Why Belief Matters More Than Behavior

We often try to change our actions without addressing our beliefs. But Jesus always targeted the heart.

"Make the tree good and its fruit will be good." – Matthew 12:33

Behavior follows belief. Fruit grows from the root. When you believe you're a child of God—deeply loved, forgiven, and made new—you will live like it.

Your brain is designed to prioritize what it believes to be true and important. Neurologically, the reticular activating system (RAS) in your brain acts like a filter, screening out information that doesn't align with your established beliefs. If you've decided—consciously or subconsciously—that something isn't relevant or true, your brain will help you overlook it, even if it's exactly what you need.

This is why renewing your mind matters so deeply. When you choose to believe what God says about you, you're retraining your brain to focus on truth. And your emotional responses, behavioral patterns, and even subconscious filters begin to align with that truth. Your body and mind start to support what your spirit already knows: you are new.

This is where grace enters—not just as forgiveness, but as divine empowerment. Grace is God's strength working in your heart, teaching you, transforming you, and helping you walk out your new identity.

Jesus likened this to leaven—a small measure of yeast working its way through the entire batch of dough. Truth, once believed, begins to spread quietly but powerfully through every area of your life. It infiltrates your reactions, heals your relationships, reshapes your thinking, and eventually overrides the lies trauma once etched into your soul.

You don't have to be perfect. You just have to keep feeding your heart the truth. Keep nurturing the wheat, and in time, the fruit will prove the seed.

Jesus gave us insight into heart transformation in the parable of the wheat and tares (Matthew 13:24–30). When asked if the weeds (tares) should be pulled up, the master said no—because uprooting them could harm the wheat. Instead, let both grow together until harvest.

This is a picture of the heart: the truth (wheat) and lies (tares) may exist at the same time for a season. But the key is not obsessing over eradicating all lies at once. The key is to nurture the truth. Tend the wheat. Feed your heart with God's Word and love. As truth takes deeper root, it will crowd out the lies.

That's why belief matters more than behavior. You don't overcome sin by hyper-focusing on sin. You overcome by focusing on your righteousness in Christ. The transformation process will take care of the lies, not through striving, but through abiding.

So the real question is: what do you believe about yourself?

How to Begin the Transformation

If you're ready to change what you believe about yourself—down to your core—here's a heart-based transformation path you can follow. Remember, the goal is to believe the truth that is already true. The goal is not to dig into your psyche to find lies, those will emerge as you intend to be persuaded of God's promises, view of you, and the truth of His nature and heart toward you.

1. Identify the truth in God's Word you want to believe.

Search scripture for what God says about that area.

If the lie is *"I'll never be enough,"* find verses that say:

* You are complete in Christ (Colossians 2:10)
* You are God's workmanship (Ephesians 2:10)
* He has given you everything you need for life and godliness (2 Peter 1:3)

Write these verses in the first person. Meditate on them. Speak them aloud.

2. Notice any contradictions in your heart's beliefs to God's truth.

Take time in prayer and reflection. As you are sowing

the truth in your mind and heart, as contradictions or objections emerge, ask yourself:

* What do I say to myself in private?
* What emotion rises when I try to believe the truth?
* Is there a recurring fear, shame, or narrative that plays out in my decisions?

Be honest. Let your heart speak. Don't condemn yourself—listen like you're gathering data.

3. Let the truth confront the lie.

As you meditate on the Word, your heart will often push back. This is good.

That tension is the Word exposing what needs healing. When you feel emotional resistance, lean in. Let the Spirit reveal where the lie took root.

Ask the Holy Spirit: *"Where did I first believe this?"*

He may show you a memory, a wound, or a conversation.

Then ask: *"Jesus, what do You want to say to me about this?"*

Let His love reframe the moment.

4. Bring the lie to the cross.

Remind your heart that Jesus died to remove not just your sin, but your shame, pain, and broken identity.

* *Surely He has borne our griefs and carried our sorrows... and by His stripes we are healed* (Isaiah 53:4–5)

* *God made Him who knew no sin to be sin for us, that we might become the righteousness of God in Him* (2 Corinthians 5:21)

Jesus absorbed every false identity you ever carried. He endured rejection so you could be accepted. See Him on the cross, taking your shame and giving you His wholeness.

5. Put on the new.

Now that you've identified the lie and brought it to the cross, it's time to put on the truth.

Ephesians 4:24 says to *"put on the new self, created to be like God in true righteousness and holiness."*

Declare the truth over yourself:

* "I am loved. I am chosen. I am whole. I am free."

* "I have a new heart, and I live from it."

* "I am not a victim of my past—I'm a child of God, empowered by grace."

Speak it. Journal it. Imagine it. Let it saturate your thinking. Repetition and reflection help engrave it into your heart.

6. Be patient with your process.

Transformation is not overnight—it's like a seed growing, or leaven spreading through dough. But it is real and lasting. Don't be discouraged by days that feel hard. Return to the truth. Keep sowing. Keep nurturing the wheat.

You can adapt this process to different beliefs and different areas of life you want to experience healing. Get into the Word of God and craft for yourself a healing series of passages that reveal God's heart for you and speak to who you now are in Christ. Always look to Christ death, burial, and resurrection. Anything healing you need to experience is addressed in some facet of His perfect life to fulfill the law in you and become your sin offering, or in his suffering on the cross, or in His victorious resurrection. Anything and everything you need is found somewhere in those events, and the power of it working in you.

God is faithful to finish what He starts in you. This is not about fixing yourself. This is about uncovering who you already are in Christ.

Your new heart already agrees with God. It already loves righteousness and desires truth. Your part is to renew your mind and let your beliefs catch up to your identity.

When your heart starts to believe the truth, everything changes—your choices, your emotions, your confidence, your intimacy with God. That's why this chapter matters. It's the turning point from brokenness to wholeness.

You are not who they said you were. You are not who the pain tried to convince you to be.

You are who God says you are—and it's time to believe it.

Reflection

* Do I believe God is safe to be close to?

* Where have I experienced rejection that might still influence how I relate to Him?

* What would intimacy with God look like for me, if I believed He truly delighted in me?

Confession

God, You are not like the ones who hurt me.

You are gentle and kind. You're not pushing me away—you're drawing me close.

I was made to walk with You. And I say yes to that again.

> **Prayer**
> Father, I've felt distant. Maybe I've been afraid of intimacy because of past wounds. But I see now—You're not like them. You're not cold or rejecting. You're full of mercy. Thank You for taking my rejection on the cross. Thank You for making space for me in Your family. I open my heart. Help me learn how to walk closely with You, without fear. I want to know You deeply, and be known by You fully.
> Amen.

PART 3
THE WORD IN THE HEART HEALING FROM THE INSIDE OUT

CHOSEN AND LOVED

Letting truth do what trauma tried to prevent.

There's a point in every transformation journey where information must become revelation. It's not enough to know what the Bible says—we have to let the truth of God's Word be planted in our hearts, take root, and grow. That's what this part of the journey is all about: planting the Word in the soil of your heart so that healing and transformation rise from the inside out. The Word of God isn't just letters on a page, the Word of God is Christ's healing presence in you. Christ is the Logos, He is the living Word of God in you to bring wisdom, revelation, and healing to make you whole.

If you've lived through trauma, loss, or rejection, chances are those experiences wrote something deep into your identity. Not just thoughts, but beliefs—about God, yourself, and your place in the world. Beliefs like, "I'll always be overlooked," or "I'm hard to love," or "God is disappointed in me." These aren't just passing emotions—they're heart-level convictions shaped by pain.

But here's the good news: your heart is no longer the old heart you once had. When you were born again, God gave you a new heart—a heart capable of receiving truth. And while old beliefs may still be trying to run your life, they don't define your identity. They just need to be replaced. Not through striving, but through seed.

Jesus said the Word of God is like a seed, and your heart is the soil (Luke 8:11–15). When you plant that seed with intention and nurture it with repetition and faith, it grows. Slowly at first. Silently. But inevitably. As truth takes root, it begins to displace the old lies, rewriting the beliefs that once kept you stuck.

Trauma tries to build walls and reinforce false narratives. But God's Word is a living force. It pierces through the soul and spirit, dividing truth from lie, discerning what's really going on inside you (Hebrews 4:12). And it doesn't just expose what's broken—it brings healing. God doesn't show you wounds to shame you; He reveals them so He can heal them.

This part of your journey will walk you through how to plant the Word in your heart, how to let it reveal what needs healing, and how to cooperate with God as He rewrites your inner world. If you'll let the truth go deep, it will do what trauma tried to prevent: it will restore you, rebuild you, and reconnect you to the joy of knowing who you truly are in Christ.

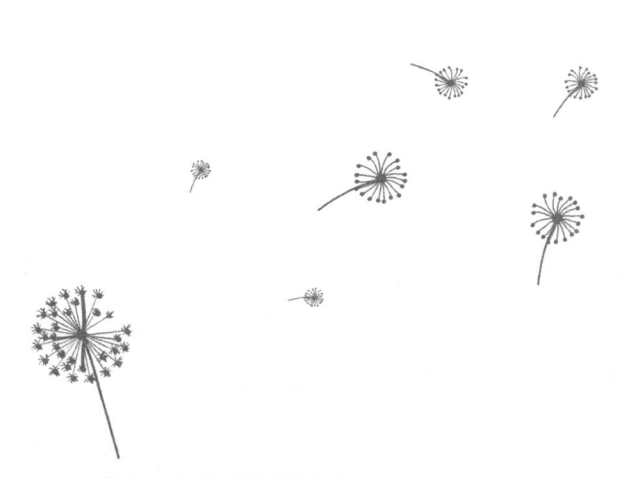

CHAPTER 7:
LETTING THE WORD DISCERN YOUR HEART

> *Transformation begins with honesty—Spirit-led, Word-revealed honesty.*

One of the most powerful and gentle ways God transforms us is through His Word. Not just reading it for knowledge, but allowing it to read us—to reveal what's really going on beneath the surface.

Hebrews 4:12 says:
"For the word of God is living and powerful, and sharper than

any two-edged sword, piercing even to the division of soul and spirit... and is a discerner of the thoughts and intents of the heart."

This isn't about self-condemnation or obsessive introspection. It's about surrendering your inner world to the truth and letting God shine His light on anything that doesn't belong. The Word of God doesn't just expose—it heals. It divides between what's of the Spirit and what's of the soul, between what's true and what's trauma.

You Don't Have to Search Alone

Looking within can feel overwhelming, especially when past wounds or lies still echo in the heart. But when you invite God's Word into your inner world, you're not alone in the search. The Holy Spirit walks with you. He doesn't come with accusation—He comes with help. He is your Comforter, your Counselor, and your guide into all truth. You're not trying to identify the lie, you're trying too believe the truth. If a lie arises as you seek to sow the truth, let it emerge, run its course emotionally, send it away in your thoughts, and choose the truth you will put on, until you feel it, and believe it.

In those vulnerable moments, when a verse brings up something painful or confronts a deep insecurity, it's easy to want to shut down or look away. But that's the very moment to be brave. Find the courage to see what your heart really believes about you—and speak truth into it. Not with condemnation, but with compassion and authority.

Speak to your heart: *"This may be how I feel, but it is not who I am. I am who God says I am."* And then decide—right there in that moment—not later, not when you feel ready, but now—to put on the truth.

The moment something painful surfaces, He is right there, not to shame you, but to show you the truth that will set you free. His grace gently applies healing where pain once ruled. His light doesn't come to blind or punish—it comes to illuminate the truth so you can walk in it.

Imagine sitting quietly with Psalm 139:14: *"I praise You because I am fearfully and wonderfully made."* You speak it aloud, and your heart tightens. Thoughts surface: "That can't be true about me... I've always felt like a mistake." That internal reaction is a signal—not of failure, but of opportunity. The Word is working. The Spirit is leading. Now healing can begin.

This is not a journey of isolation—it's intimacy with the

God who sees and understands you fully.

What the Word Will Reveal

When the Word begins to interact with your heart, several layers of belief may come to the surface:

* **Lies you've believed about yourself** — *"I'm a burden. I'm not wanted. I'll never change."* These lies often formed in childhood or trauma and became internal narratives.

* **Misunderstandings about God** — *"He's distant. He's disappointed. He's punishing me."* These distortions usually reflect how we've been treated by others, not how God actually is.

* **Emotional wounds that still hurt** — rejection, shame, fear, abandonment, betrayal—all of which create protective layers that resist intimacy and healing.

As you meditate on scriptures like Romans 8:1 — *"There is therefore now no condemnation for those who are in Christ Jesus"* — you might notice immediate inner conflict. You may feel condemned. Your mind may argue, *"But I've failed too many times."* Your emotions may say, *"That can't be for me."*

That moment of disagreement is sacred. It's not evidence

you're doing something wrong—it's proof the Word is reading your heart. The Bible is showing you both your true image and where trauma or deception has tried to distort it.

How to Let the Word Discern Your Heart

This is not a mechanical routine but a relational experience—your heart communing with God through His truth. To engage the Word in this way:

1. Choose a theme or truth you want to grow in (e.g., *"I am chosen," "I am safe," "God delights in me"*).

2. Find 5–10 scriptures that express that truth clearly. Write them in a journal.

3. Read each verse slowly, out loud, listening with your heart.

4. After each verse, pause and ask:

* *What did I feel as I read that?*
* *Do I believe this right now?*
* *What memory or emotion comes to mind as I hear this?*

5. Journal what rises—without judgment. Let your heart speak honestly.

6. Ask the Holy Spirit:

* *Where did this belief start?*

* *What is the truth You want me to receive in its place?*

7. Return daily to the truth you're planting. Let it form new roots over time.

8. Rewrite each passage in the first person, past tense, and use those rephrased passages as personal confessions for mind renewal. Connect to them emotionally. Feel and see the truth. Own it as your identity. Not to make it true, but because it is already true of you.

Over time, the Word begins to shape your internal world. Even when your thoughts or emotions don't yet line up, the Word anchors you in God's truth. Psalm 119:105 says, "Your word is a lamp to my feet and a light to my path." It will light your next step and gently carry you forward.

This is how transformation becomes sustainable—by continually letting God's true image of you become your own self-image. The Word doesn't just show you what's wrong; it reveals who you truly are.

This Is Not Self-Help—It's Heart Help

You're not trying to fix yourself. You're yielding to the One who already made you new. The world says, "Look inward and try harder." The Kingdom says, "Behold Christ and believe."

God is not asking you to perform surgery on your soul. He's asking you to rest under His Word like sunlight and let it warm, expose, and restore. As you behold the truth, grace begins its work. Your heart softens. Your mind renews. Your behavior eventually follows.

James 1:23–25 speaks of looking into the Word as a mirror. The Word shows you what kind of person you are—your true identity in Christ. And when you stay with it—not forgetting what you've seen—it begins to shape how you think, feel, and act.

The Word reflects the real you—made new in Christ. But it also reflects what you believe about yourself that's still being healed. That tension is where grace meets you. It's not failure—it's formation.

The Word of God is not an academic textbook or a religious rulebook—it is alive. It knows you. It searches your heart with perfect love. And it reveals what's in you, not to disqualify you, but to align you with who you really are.

Every time you open it, it opens you. Every time you engage it honestly, it reveals something beautiful: a truth planted by God before the world began, waiting to be believed.

So keep showing up. Keep letting it read you. Keep letting the truth displace the lies. Until the Word planted in your heart bears fruit in every part of your life.

Reflection

* Am I afraid of what I might discover in my heart?

* Do I trust the Word of God and the Spirit of God to be gentle with my story?

* What's one belief I want to examine with God's help this week?

* What is a scripture that recently didn't feel true to me? What surfaced when I read it?

* Am I willing to speak truth to myself in the middle of the discomfort?

First-Person Confession

God's Word is alive in me. It sees me, knows me, and loves me.

I am not afraid of what's inside—I trust the Spirit to guide me.

I open my heart to the truth. I let the Word do its work.

Lies are being exposed. Truth is being planted.

I am being transformed from the inside out.

> ### Prayer
> Father, thank You for giving me a new heart and a renewed mind. Thank You for Your Word, which sees into the deepest parts of me—not to condemn, but to heal. I trust You. I welcome Your light.
> Holy Spirit, guide me as I reflect. Help me recognize every lie and let go of every false belief. Speak clearly as I meditate on Your promises. Let Your Word break through old strongholds and bring lasting transformation. I believe the truth is stronger than any lie, and I receive it now with joy.
> Thank You for loving me enough to lead me into freedom.
> In Jesus' name, amen.

CHAPTER 8:
BRINGING THE LIE TO THE CROSS

> *What you believe must pass through what Jesus finished.*

Once a lie is exposed in your heart, you stand at a powerful turning point. You've named the belief. You've felt the emotions it stirs. You've seen how it conflicts with what God says. Now it's time to bring that lie into the only place where real change happens—the cross.

The cross is more than just a symbol of Christianity. It is the epicenter of your identity. Every lie, every wound, every failure, every form of rejection met its end in the death of Jesus. And every promise, every healing, every truth about who you are was resurrected with Him. It's where your brokenness was met with His wholeness, your shame was buried, and your true self was raised to new life.

Many people treat the cross like a starting point—something they pass through once at salvation. But the truth is, the cross is not just the entry gate to your faith. It is the place you return to again and again, to trade broken beliefs for divine truth. It's where you exchange the things that hurt you for the healing that already belongs to you. The cross is God's statement of eternal love and justice, His intervention in your story, and His validation of your worth.

You don't bring your lie to the cross because God needs you to. You bring it because your heart needs to see that the pain has already been addressed. That's where real peace and transformation begin. You are not making something happen—you are aligning with what Jesus already finished.

Why the Cross Matters for Your Heart

You can't just argue a lie out of your soul. You must

replace it with something stronger, something eternal—something that carries the full weight of heaven's authority. That's what the cross offers. It is God's final statement over your pain, your past, and your personhood. It is the place where every accusation falls silent and the voice of love speaks louder than shame.

Your heart will not be transformed by willpower or religious effort. It will only be transformed by what Jesus accomplished on your behalf. At the cross, God didn't just offer forgiveness—He offered identity restoration. Every place where trauma tried to define you, Jesus stepped in to redefine you. Every place sin tried to label you, Jesus rewrote your story with His own blood.

When you bring the lie to the cross, you're not denying the pain—it's real. You're not pretending the betrayal or trauma didn't happen. Instead, you're choosing to place it where healing has already been purchased. You're letting the finished work of Jesus take precedence over your unfinished places.

This is not emotional suppression. It's divine exchange. The cross holds the power to break the cycle because it severed the root. The more clearly you see what Jesus bore for you, the more deeply your heart can let go of the lies it has clung to. You no longer need to carry what

He already carried. You no longer need to prove your worth when He already proved it on Calvary.

Jesus didn't just die to sin and the power of death for you—He died as you. He became sin so that you might become the righteousness of God (2 Corinthians 5:21). He was rejected so you could be accepted. He was shamed so you could be honored. He bore the curse so you could inherit the blessing. That's what the cross offers. It is God's final statement over your pain, your past, and your personhood. When you bring the lie to the cross, you're not denying the pain—it's real. You're just refusing to let it define you anymore.

Isaiah 53 tells us what He carried:

* Our griefs and sorrows
* Our transgressions and iniquities
* Our chastisement and wounds

And it also tells us what He gave us:

* Peace
* Healing
* Righteousness

This is the great exchange: you bring what's broken, and

He gives what's whole. It's not theoretical—it's deeply personal. It's not just about the cross as history. It's about your story being rewritten in Christ.

How to Bring the Lie to the Cross

This isn't a quick process that will happen as you read the words on this page. You'll need to sit with it and reflect. You'll need to relax, take some deep breaths, open your heart, and let Him see you.

1. Identify the Lie Clearly

Write it down exactly how you believe it, even if it sounds irrational: *"I'm always left out. I'm too much. I'll never be healed."* Honesty is the first step toward freedom.

2. Feel It Honestly

Sit with the emotion. Don't rush past the pain. Let it rise, knowing you're safe in God's presence. Jesus is not afraid of your tears—He weeps with those who weep. Acknowledge that it's just a memory, and it's just an emotion.

3. Find the Truth That Contradicts the Lie

Search the Word. What does God say about this? Maybe it's Romans 8:1, *"There is now no condemnation,"* or

Ephesians 1:4, *"You are chosen and blameless in His sight."* This is the truth that carries the weight to shift your identity.

4. Look to the Cross

Ask, *Where did Jesus already deal with this?* If it's shame, He bore it when stripped and mocked. If it's fear, He faced it sweating blood in Gethsemane. If it's abandonment, He cried out, *"Why have You forsaken Me?"*

5. Speak the Exchange

Out loud, declare: *"I give You this lie, Jesus. I give You the pain. I receive Your truth in its place."* Let your words match heaven's verdict over you. And intend to feel His healing embrace.

6. Put On the Truth

Just as you would put on clothing, clothe yourself in the identity Christ purchased for you. Say it. Imagine it. Believe it anew. Do it now, not later. Don't wait to feel different—speak and step into your truth by faith.

This is not a formula—it's a moment of surrender. It's where your trauma ends and truth takes over.

Additional Examples of Putting On the Truth

Lie: *"I'll never be free from this addiction or habit."*

Truth: *Romans 6:6 – "Our old self was crucified with Him... so that we would no longer be enslaved to sin."*

Exchange: *"Jesus, I give You the belief that I'm stuck. At the cross, You broke sin's power over me. I am free in You. In You, I am no longer a slave to sin but alive to righteousness."*

Lie: *"I'm not good enough to be used by God."*

Truth: *2 Corinthians 5:17 – "If anyone is in Christ, he is a new creation; the old has passed away."*

Exchange: *"Father, I give You the feeling that I'm disqualified. In Christ, I am made new. I am equipped and called. In Him, I am created for good works, and I walk in them."*

Lie: *"God is disappointed in me."*

Truth: *Colossians 1:22 – "He has reconciled you by Christ's physical body through death to present you holy in His sight, without blemish and free from accusation."*

Exchange: *"Jesus, I give You my fear of Your disappointment. You carried my guilt and made me blameless. In You, I stand accepted and righteous. I am not condemned—I am celebrated."*

Lie: *"I'll always struggle with anxiety."*

Truth: *Philippians 4:7 – "The peace of God, which surpasses all understanding, will guard your hearts and your minds in Christ Jesus."*

Exchange: *"Lord, I bring You my anxious thoughts. On the cross, You bore my chastisement to give me peace. In You, I receive rest and security. I put on the mind of Christ and walk in peace."*

Lie: *"I'm broken beyond repair."*

Truth: *Ephesians 2:10 – "For we are God's workmanship, created in Christ Jesus for good works."*

Exchange: *"Jesus, I give You this belief that I am too far gone. In You, I am Your masterpiece. I am made whole. I am restored and beautiful in Your sight."*

Lie: *"My needs are too much for anyone to care about."*

Truth: *Philippians 4:19 – "My God shall supply all your need according to His riches in glory by Christ Jesus."*

Exchange: *"Father, I bring You the fear that I'm a burden. At the cross, Jesus bore my loneliness. In Him, I am seen, valued, and cared for. My needs matter to You."*

Lie: *"No one could ever truly love me."*

Truth: *Romans 5:8 – "God demonstrates His love for us in this: while we were still sinners, Christ died for us."*

Exchange: *"Jesus, I give You the belief that I'm unlovable. At the cross, You proved my worth. In You, I am deeply loved with an everlasting love."*

Each of these lies finds its end at the cross. And each truth is established in your new identity in Him. You are not trying to become something different—you are awakening to who you already are in Christ.

The cross is not a one-time fix but a continual invitation. Every time a lie rises, you know where to take it. The cross isn't just where Jesus died—it's where your old identity died too. You don't live there anymore.

This practice becomes a rhythm: name the lie, feel the emotion, bring it to the cross, receive the truth, put on the new man. Again and again. Until truth has replaced the lie at the deepest level of your identity.

Let the cross speak louder than your pain. Let Jesus define you more than your past. Let grace rebuild what trauma tried to destroy.

Reflection

* What lie have I believed that still affects my emotions or behavior?

* What truth from Scripture contradicts that lie?

* What aspect of the cross shows me Jesus has already dealt with this for me?

First-Person Confession

Jesus, I believe You took my pain. You bore my shame. You carried my rejection.

I no longer agree with the lie. I no longer identify with the hurt.

I receive the truth of who I am in You—accepted, whole, and new.

The cross is where the lie ends and my freedom begins.

Prayer

Father, thank You for sending Jesus to bear my pain and take my place. You saw me in my confusion and trauma and still called me worthy of redemption. Jesus, I bring this lie to You. I lay it at the cross. I trust You've already dealt with it fully.

Help me now to receive Your truth—not just in theory, but deep in my heart. Let it reshape my identity and restore my peace. I choose today to believe what You say about me. I choose to walk in freedom.

In Your name, Jesus, amen.

CHAPTER 9:
PUTTING ON THE NEW MAN

Living from who you are, not who you were.

The moment you bring a lie to the cross and receive the truth in its place, something sacred happens. You've made an exchange: your false identity for God's truth about you. But you're not finished. Now, you must wear that truth. You must put on the new man—the version of you that Jesus raised up with Himself.

This phrase "put on the new man" comes from Ephesians 4:22–24:

"...put off your old self, which belongs to your former manner of life and is corrupt through deceitful desires, and be renewed in the spirit of your minds, and put on the new self, created after the likeness of God in true righteousness and holiness."

To "put on" the new man means to live from your new nature—not by trying harder, but by aligning your thoughts, emotions, and actions with who you truly are in Christ. This is about identity first, then transformation. You're not trying to become holy; you've already been made holy in Christ. Now you're learning to think and act like the new creation you already are.

Putting on the new man doesn't mean faking it until you make it. It means training your heart and mind to believe what's true, so that you naturally live out of that truth. It's stepping into the wardrobe of heaven and choosing to dress yourself in what Jesus purchased for you—righteousness, peace, power, love, and purpose.

This is a lifestyle shift. The old way of living—striving, proving, performing—is over. The new way of living is resting in your identity and responding to God's grace. The more you clothe yourself in truth, the more your thoughts, habits, and reactions will align with your true self.

Identity Before Behavior

God's method is always identity before behavior. He doesn't ask you to live holy so that you'll be righteous. He declares you righteous so that you can live holy.

This is a major shift from how many people try to grow spiritually. Instead of starting from a place of acceptance, they begin from insecurity. Instead of resting in the finished work of Christ, they try to earn their way into worthiness. But transformation doesn't come from performance—it comes from belief.

When you were born again, God didn't just forgive you—He recreated you. You are now a new creation (2 Corinthians 5:17). That means the core of who you are is new. Your old self—your shame-filled, fear-driven, sin-bound self—was crucified with Christ. The new you is righteous, accepted, and empowered.

This new identity isn't just a spiritual label—it's your internal reality. Your spirit is one with Christ. Your heart has been made new. God has written His law on your heart and given you a nature that wants what He wants. The struggle isn't about becoming something you're not—it's about shedding the lies that keep you from living as who you truly are.

Putting on the new man/woman is choosing to believe that what God says about you is more true than how you feel. It's saying, *"Even when my emotions tell me otherwise, I will choose the truth. Even when my circumstances contradict it, I will walk by faith, not by sight."* That's how transformation takes root—from the inside out.

You've Already Been Made New

The foundation of your healing and transformation is this unshakable truth: *you already are new in Christ.* This isn't something you're working toward—it's something you're learning to live from.

2 Corinthians 5:17 says,

> *"If anyone is in Christ, he is a new creation. Old things have passed away; behold, all things have become new."*

At the moment of salvation, you didn't just get forgiven—you were recreated. God didn't patch up the old you. He birthed a new you. Your spirit was made alive with His life. You were made righteous, holy, and blameless in His sight—not by behavior, but by birth.

But this truth must be put on. You can be completely new in spirit, but still think, feel, and act like the old version of yourself if your mind isn't renewed. This is why Paul urges us in Ephesians 4:22–24:

> *"Put off... the old man, which is corrupt... and be renewed in the spirit of your mind, and put on the new man, created according to God, in true righteousness and holiness."*

"Put on" is not a metaphor for pretending. It's a command to align with your true nature. Like putting on clothes, it's a conscious choice. You clothe yourself in truth, identity, and wholeness—even when you don't feel like it. Especially when you don't feel like it.

Putting on the new man means taking God's word about you more seriously than your feelings, your history, or others' opinions. It means walking into every room—into every memory—with the awareness that you are who God says you are.

This Is a Daily Choice

Putting on the new man is not a one-time event. It's a daily, relational, intentional rhythm. You're not earning anything—you're learning how to live in what you've already received.

Each day, you'll be presented with opportunities to either respond from your old programming or from your renewed identity. Will you respond to rejection by retreating in fear, or by standing in the truth that you're already accepted by God? Will you see yourself through the lens of failure, or through the victory Jesus already secured for you?

Here's what it might look like in everyday life:

* **You feel insecure walking into a meeting.**
  Instead of rehearsing your inadequacy, you whisper: *"I am complete in Christ. I carry His wisdom and peace."*

* **You feel triggered by rejection in a relationship.**
  You pause, breathe, and declare: *"I am chosen, not rejected. God delights in me, and I will not agree with shame."*

* **You struggle with temptation or old habits.**
  Rather than spiraling into guilt, you speak: *"Sin is no longer my master. I'm dead to sin and alive to God."*

You may not feel instant change—but you are training your heart to believe the truth. You're creating new spiritual and neural pathways. You are strengthening your inner man through consistency, not perfection.

This is how grace works: God gives you a new heart, and then empowers you to live from it. Your part is to choose agreement. His part is to bring transformation.

Examples of Putting On the New Man in Real Life

Putting on the new man is not vague spiritual theory—it's deeply practical. It means replacing old thought patterns with the truth of your identity in Christ, moment by moment. Here are some real-life examples of how this works:

1. Lie: "I'll always be broken."

What surfaces: You feel hopeless and overwhelmed by emotional pain or repeated mistakes.

Put on truth:
"I am healed by His wounds (Isaiah 53:5). I have been made whole in Christ (Colossians 2:10). The Spirit of the Lord is within me to bind up the brokenhearted and make me new (Luke 4:18)."

Anchor verse: *"He who began a good work in me will be faithful to complete it" (Philippians 1:6).*

2. Lie: "I'm too damaged to be loved."

What surfaces: A feeling of deep shame and fear that no one, especially God, could accept you.

Put on truth:
"I am accepted in the Beloved (Ephesians 1:6). I am fearfully and

wonderfully made (Psalm 139:14). Nothing can separate me from the love of God (Romans 8:38–39)."

Anchor truth from the cross: *Jesus bore your rejection so you could be adopted (Isaiah 53:3, Galatians 4:5).*

3. Lie: "I'll never overcome this sin."

What surfaces: You feel stuck in a cycle and powerless.

Put on truth:

"Sin shall not have dominion over me, for I am not under law but under grace (Romans 6:14). I am crucified with Christ—it is no longer I who live but Christ lives in me (Galatians 2:20). I have power, love, and a sound mind (2 Timothy 1:7)."

Resurrection identity: You were raised with Christ to walk in newness of life (Romans 6:4).

4. Lie: "I'm a failure. I always mess things up."

What surfaces: Harsh self-criticism, anxiety, or avoidance.

Put on truth:

"I am God's workmanship, created in Christ Jesus for good works (Ephesians 2:10). I can do all things through Christ who strengthens me (Philippians 4:13). The righteous may fall seven times but rise again (Proverbs 24:16)."

Putting on the Word Is Putting on Christ

Romans 13:14 says, *"Put on the Lord Jesus Christ, and make no provision for the flesh."*

When you put on the truth about who you are in Christ, you're not just trying to improve yourself—you are putting on Christ Himself. You're aligning your soul with what's already true in your spirit.

You're saying, *"I choose to believe I am righteous, not because of my performance, but because Jesus gave me His righteousness. I choose to act like a son or daughter, not a slave. I choose love over fear. I choose the finished work over shame."*

This isn't behavior modification. It's identity revelation. And it's made possible by grace, not striving.

This Is the True You

As you continue to put on the new man, the fruit will come. Love. Joy. Peace. Patience. Confidence. Clarity. You don't have to force it—you simply abide in the truth.

And if you mess up? You return to the truth again. You don't spiral. You don't re-identify with the old man. You look back to the cross, remember who you are, and keep going.

Putting on the new man is how you behold your identity until it becomes your reflex. Until the truth becomes your inner narrative. Until the Word reshapes your entire self-image.

You're not faking anything. You're finally being who you really are.

Reflection

* In what area of life do I still respond like the "old me"?

* What lie might be driving that response?

* What truth has God spoken that I can begin to put on today?

* What would it look like to walk into that situation as the new man or woman in Christ?

First-Person Confession

I am a new creation in Christ.

My old self was crucified with Him, and I now live by faith in the Son of God.

I am not ruled by fear, shame, or sin—I am empowered by grace.

I put off the lies and put on the truth.

I wear the righteousness, love, and power of Jesus like a robe.

I live from the Spirit, and I walk in the Spirit.

I am who God says I am—and I walk like it today.

> **Prayer**
> Father, thank You for making me new. I don't always feel new, but I choose to believe what You've said over what I feel. You gave me a new heart, a new spirit, and a new identity— and I receive it.
> Holy Spirit, help me put off the old lies and patterns that no longer belong to me. Help me remember who I am in every situation.
> I put on the new man—created in true righteousness and holiness. I put on Jesus Himself.
> Thank You that I'm not pretending—I'm becoming. I trust You to complete this transformation in me, one step at a time.
> In Jesus' name, amen.

PART 4:
LETTING THE WORD REVEAL THE HEART

Transformation begins where truth meets honesty.

By now, you've begun to see that real change doesn't come from trying harder—it comes from believing differently. And belief isn't just an idea in the mind—it's written on the heart. If trauma, rejection, or repeated failure has shaped your identity, then what your heart believes about God, yourself, and your future may not yet align with the truth.

That's why God gave us His Word—not only to teach us, but to read us.

Hebrews 4:12 says:
"For the word of God is living and active... it judges the thoughts and attitudes of the heart."

In this part of the journey, you'll learn how to let the Word of God do its deepest work—exposing lies, confronting wounds, and anchoring you in truth. But this is not about harsh self-examination. It's about Spirit-led honesty. It's about allowing the One who loves you most to guide you through the inner places where old beliefs still speak.

You'll discover how to engage the Word with your heart wide open—letting it show you what you've really believed and helping you make the exchange. When you see the lie, you'll learn how to bring it to the cross. When you encounter the truth, you'll practice putting it on. Not through striving, but through grace.

This part of the book will walk you step by step into the heart of transformation: not self-help, but heart-help—by the Word, through the Spirit, grounded in the finished work of Jesus.

Let the Word reveal. Let the truth replace. Let your heart be renewed. This is where healing becomes identity, and identity becomes a way of life.

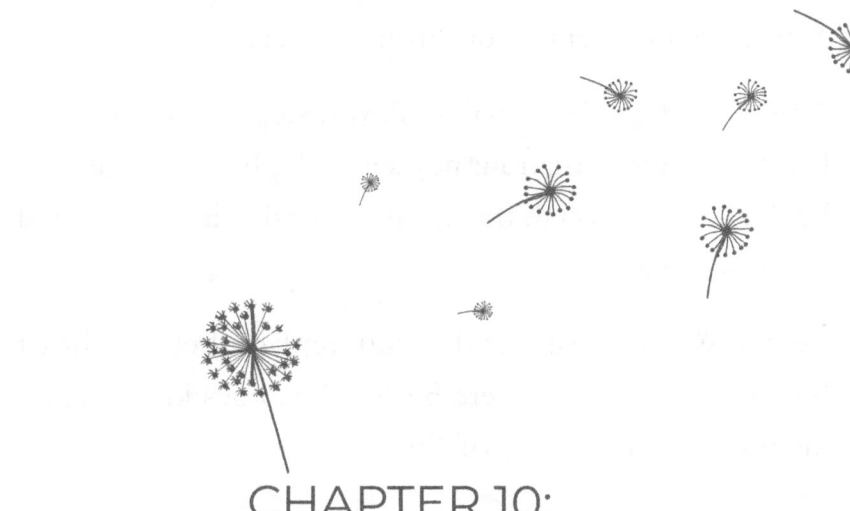

CHAPTER 10:
THE WORD DISCERNS WHAT YOU BELIEVE

Let the light in—not to expose you, but to heal you.

There's a moment in every believer's journey when a scripture hits you—not because it's hard to understand, but because something in your heart resists it. Maybe it's a verse you've heard your whole life. You know it's true. But it just doesn't feel true—not for you.

You read *"There is therefore now no condemnation for those who are in Christ Jesus"* (Romans 8:1), and instead of comfort, a knot rises in your stomach. Thoughts echo inside: *"Not after what I've done… God may forgive others, but I still carry guilt."*

That moment—when the Word contradicts your feelings—is one of the holiest moments in your healing journey. Because that's where God meets you. That's where the light of truth gently confronts the shadows of false belief. And it's where freedom begins.

This is not about being *"caught"* or *"exposed"* by God in a negative sense. It's about finally seeing what's been hidden in your heart so He can heal it. His light doesn't come to humiliate—it comes to restore. And He never shows you a lie without offering the truth to replace it.

What You Truly Believe—Not Just What You Know

Many of us have been discipled into thinking that right knowledge equals transformation. But knowing something in your head isn't the same as believing it with your heart.

You can quote *"God loves me"* all day long, but if a deep wound from your past says *"I'm unlovable,"* your emotions will side with the wound every time. That doesn't mean the truth isn't working—it means your heart needs time, honesty, and grace to catch up.

Romans 10:10 says, *"With the heart one believes unto righteousness."* Belief isn't mental agreement—it's the deep place where identity is formed and actions take root. And the heart learns differently than the mind. It learns by what's repeated, by what's emotional, and by what feels personally meaningful.

Trauma, rejection, and failure can all write powerful stories on the heart—stories that may be completely untrue but feel like reality. That's why it's not enough to memorize scripture. We must allow the Word to read us, confront what we've believed, and rewrite the inner script.

When you open your Bible and read *"You are God's masterpiece"* (Ephesians 2:10), and your heart replies, *"I feel like a mess,"* don't stop reading. That tension is where the Spirit does His best work. Let the discomfort stay long enough to listen. Ask the Holy Spirit, *"Why doesn't this feel true? What do You want me to see here?"*

The journey of transformation is not about learning more—it's about believing better.

The Mirror That Reads You

James 1:23–25 describes the Word of God as a mirror. But it's not a mirror like the ones we use in the bathroom. This one reflects something deeper: your spirit. The real you. The one God made new when you were born again.

"Anyone who listens to the word but does not do what it says is like someone who looks at his face in a mirror and, after looking at himself, goes away and immediately forgets what he looks like." (James 1:23–24)

The Word shows you who you are in Christ. And at the same time, it shows you where you're still living out of an old identity. The gap between those two realities is where the enemy tries to attack you—but it's also where the Spirit invites you into lasting change.

When you read, *"You are seated with Christ in heavenly places"* (Ephesians 2:6), and your inner voice scoffs, *"I feel stuck on the floor,"* the mirror of the Word is showing you both what's true and what still needs renewing.

This is what it means for the Word to discern your heart. It doesn't just show you your new identity—it reveals where your current beliefs still disagree with it. Not to shame you, but to give you a chance to agree with heaven.

And here's the beautiful thing: the Word doesn't just reflect you—it transforms you. As you behold who you are in Christ, the Spirit goes to work, changing how you see yourself, how you respond, and how you live.

Examples of the Word Discerning the Heart

Scripture: *"You are fearfully and wonderfully made"* (Psalm 139:14)

Heart response: *"I don't feel wonderful. I've always felt unwanted."*

What's happening: The truth is confronting an old self-image. Don't run. Let God speak. Ask: *"What do You say about me, Lord?"*

Scripture: *"Perfect love casts out fear"* (1 John 4:18)

Heart response: *"Then why am I still afraid?"*

What's happening: A hidden belief that love is unsafe may be surfacing. Let the Spirit remind you of how Jesus demonstrated perfect love on the cross—for you.

Scripture: *"The Lord is my Shepherd; I shall not want"* (Psalm 23:1)

Heart response: *"But I'm still lacking. I don't feel taken care of."*

What's happening: A belief shaped by unmet needs or childhood lack is being challenged. You can tell the Lord, *"I want to know You as Provider. Teach my heart to trust You here."*

Every conflict between your emotions and God's Word is an invitation—not to perform, but to receive. God is not surprised by your internal resistance. He already sees it, and He's not angry. He's kind enough to bring it to the surface so you can experience real freedom.

How to Let the Word Discern Your Heart

Here's a process you can practice regularly:

1. Pick a truth you want to believe — for example: *"I am safe with God"* or *"I am fully forgiven."*

2. Find 5–10 scriptures that clearly affirm that truth. Write them out in a journal or note app.

3. Read each verse slowly, out loud. Feel it. Don't rush.

4. Notice your internal response:

* Do I feel peace or resistance?
* What emotions are stirred?
* Does this feel true to me?

5. Let your heart answer. Even if the response feels wrong or painful, let it be honest.

6. Ask God:

* Where did I learn this belief?
* What truth do You want me to receive in its place?

7. Speak the truth over yourself—with gentleness, consistency, and conviction.

8. Return to the verses daily, even if the feelings don't change right away. The Word is planting new seeds. Give it time.

You're Not Alone in This

The Holy Spirit is your counselor. He's present in these moments to guide and comfort you. You're not trying to perform. You're surrendering. You're letting light into a room that's ready to be healed.

And remember: **you're not the sum of what your heart currently believes.** You are who God says you are—even if your heart is still catching up to that truth.

Let the Word be your mirror. Let it reflect back the new creation you've become. And when it reveals the gap, don't run from it—run to the One who is closing it.

Reflection

* What recent scripture stirred discomfort or unbelief in me?

* Do I take time to slow down and let the Word speak to my heart?

* What truth about God or myself do I want to believe more deeply?

* Am I willing to let the Word confront old stories without shame?

First-Person Confession

God's Word reveals what's true about me—even when my feelings say otherwise.

I am not afraid of the truth, because truth sets me free.

I welcome the Word to read me, to love me, and to heal me.

Even when lies speak loudly, I anchor myself in what God says.

I am being transformed by the renewing of my mind.

And I say yes to that process today.

Prayer

Father, thank You for the gift of Your Word. It's not just information—it's transformation. I trust You to speak to my heart through every verse I read.

When I feel resistance, help me pause, not push away. When the old stories surface, remind me of who I am in Christ. Thank You that Your Spirit is with me, helping me discern, replace, and renew.

I open myself to be known and loved. I give You permission to search me and heal me. Your truth is stronger than my past. I receive it with a willing heart.

In Jesus' name, amen.

CHAPTER 11:
FROM EXPOSURE TO HEALING

> *God reveals what's broken—not to shame you, but to heal you.*

Transformation doesn't begin with trying harder—it begins with seeing clearly. And not just seeing the truth in Scripture, but seeing what's inside you that doesn't yet agree with it.

When you let the Word read your heart, it often exposes things you didn't even know were still there—old beliefs, silent assumptions, fears you thought you buried, shame you thought you moved on from. It can be jarring. But it's also incredibly hopeful.

Because exposure isn't judgment—it's invitation.

It's the moment the Spirit gently says, *"This belief can't go with you into freedom. Let Me help you lay it down."* That's what this chapter is about: learning how to respond when God's Word reveals a lie that's been living in your heart—and how to walk that moment all the way to healing.

The light of God doesn't come to humiliate you. It's not here to punish or embarrass. He reveals with timing, mercy, and the goal of healing. He's not dumping your past on you—He's inviting you into wholeness.

Psalm 139:23–24 says:
"Search me, O God, and know my heart; try me and know my thoughts! And see if there be any grievous way in me, and lead me in the way everlasting."

Notice the progression: Search me… See what's wrong… Then **lead me**. God doesn't just expose—He guides. Every time something broken surfaces, He is right there with the truth that will set you free.

So when something rises—an old fear, a bitter belief,

a reaction that feels bigger than the moment—don't rush past it. Don't shame yourself. Recognize: This is exposure—and healing is next.

Exposure Is a Sign of Progress

When a painful belief rises up, your first reaction might be guilt or frustration. You might think, *"I thought I was over this,"* or *"Why is this still here?"*

But exposure is proof that the Word is doing its job.

Hebrews 4:12 says the Word discerns the thoughts and intentions of the heart. That means it shines light on what's deep inside—not to crush you, but to divide what's true from what's trauma. It's the Spirit saying, *"Here's something we're ready to heal."*

Think of a wound under the skin that's been festering. When it's brought to the surface, it might look worse for a moment—but that's the first step toward healing. The exposure isn't the problem—it's the beginning of the solution.

The same is true spiritually. When a lie surfaces, it's a gift. Not a weakness. Because once it's seen, it can be brought to the cross—and replaced with truth.

Bringing the Lie to the Cross

This is the key shift. Once something false is revealed, you don't manage it or try to willpower your way out of it. You bring it to the place where it was already defeated: the cross of Christ.

"Surely He has borne our griefs and carried our sorrows... He was pierced for our transgressions... upon Him was the chastisement that brought us peace, and by His wounds we are healed."

—Isaiah 53:4–5

Jesus didn't just die for your sin. He bore your sorrow. Your false identity. Your rejection. Your fear. Your trauma.

To bring a lie to the cross means to acknowledge it, locate it in Christ's suffering, and receive the truth purchased in His resurrection. It's not just theological—it's personal. It's where your pain meets His provision.

From Trauma-Formed Belief to Cross-Based Identity

Let's say a lie surfaces like:
"I always have to perform to be accepted."

Pause. Acknowledge it. Don't rush past the emotions.

Say to God:
"This is how I feel. This is what I've believed. But I don't want to carry it anymore."

Then locate that belief in the cross:

Jesus was **rejected** so you could be **accepted**.

He was **stripped** of dignity so you could be **clothed** in righteousness.

He was **wounded** so you could be **healed.**

And now, speak the exchange:

"God, I reject the lie that I must perform to be loved. I receive the truth that I am accepted in the Beloved. I am chosen. I am secure. I am Your child."

The Word says:
"Put off the old self... and be renewed in the spirit of your mind... and put on the new self, created after the likeness of God in true righteousness and holiness."
—Ephesians 4:22–24

That's what this process is: putting off the lie, renewing your mind with truth, and putting on your new identity in Christ.

Healing Is Ongoing, But It Starts Now

The beauty of this journey is that it doesn't require perfection—just participation. Healing doesn't mean you never feel the lie again. It means that when it surfaces, you now know what to do with it.

The more you respond this way—bringing each exposed belief to the cross—the more your heart begins to believe the truth. And over time, those old lies lose their power. They get quieter. Lighter. Easier to replace. That's the work of grace.

Titus 2:11–12 says the grace of God doesn't just save you—it teaches you. It trains your heart how to live differently, how to think differently, how to trust differently.

Reflection

* What has the Word recently revealed about my inner beliefs?

* Am I allowing the Spirit to lead me from exposure to healing?

* What lie am I ready to bring to the cross today?

* What truth has God already made available to replace it?

First-Person Confession

God, when You expose a lie in me, it's not to shame me—it's to heal me.

You are not afraid of my brokenness.

You invite me into transformation.

I bring every false belief to the cross.

I receive the truth of who I am in Christ.

I walk in the freedom Jesus purchased for me.

Prayer

Father, thank You for revealing what needs healing. You never expose to condemn—but to restore. When the Word shines light on my pain, I won't run or hide. I'll bring it to You. I'll trust the cross. I'll make the exchange.

Jesus, thank You for bearing not just my sin, but the pain and beliefs that came with it. You've carried my sorrow. You've borne my shame. You've absorbed every accusation—and given me truth in its place.

Holy Spirit, help me recognize the lies when they surface. Remind me of who I am. Strengthen me to put off the old and put on the new. Teach me to walk in truth until it feels like home.

I trust You. I receive Your healing love.
In Jesus' name—Amen.

PART 5:
WALKING WITH GOD THROUGH RENEWAL

Beholding truth. Becoming whole.

You were made for more than survival. You were made for daily connection with the One who created you, redeemed you, and delights in you. All the transformation you've experienced so far—everything God has revealed, healed, and spoken—isn't the end. It's the beginning of a renewed relationship with Him. One rooted in love, led by truth, and empowered by grace.

God didn't just want to fix your brokenness. He wanted to walk with you in wholeness.

This part of your journey is about integration—learning to live with the truth fully planted in your heart. You've seen lies exposed and old beliefs surrendered. Now it's time to walk in your new identity and stay close to the One who made you new.

Paul writes in 2 Corinthians 3:18,
"But we all, with unveiled face, beholding as in a mirror the glory of the Lord, are being transformed into the same image from glory to glory, just as by the Spirit of the Lord."

Transformation happens in the gaze. Not in striving. Not in self-fixing. But in beholding the truth—again and again—until your heart fully believes it and your life reflects it.

CHOSEN AND LOVED

In this final section, we'll walk through the rhythms that keep you grounded in your new identity. You'll learn how to keep putting on the truth, how to respond when old lies try to return, and how to keep your heart sensitive and connected to God's voice.

This is a lifelong relationship of renewal—not a religious duty, but a love journey. He's not rushing you. He's walking with you. And every day you say yes to truth, you're becoming more fully who you've always been in His eyes.

Let's keep going—together.

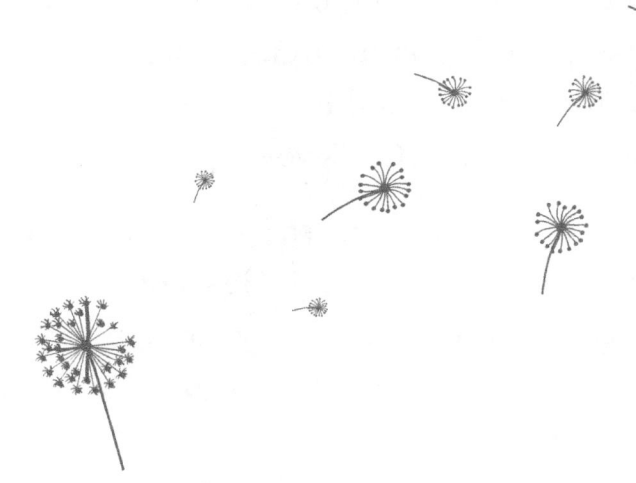

CHAPTER 12:
EPHESIANS 4:22–24 IN PRACTICE

> *A daily rhythm of renewal—putting off, being renewed, and putting on.*

Transformation isn't a one-time event. It's not an emotional moment or a mental breakthrough, although those things help. Real change is a daily practice—rooted in grace, guided by the Spirit, and empowered by the Word. That's what Paul outlines so clearly in Ephesians 4.

"Put off your former way of life, your old self, which is corrupted

by deceitful desires; be renewed in the spirit of your minds; and put on the new self, created after the likeness of God in true righteousness and holiness."

—Ephesians 4:22–24

This passage gives us the most direct, practical framework for living out our new identity. Not by obsessing over the old self, but by putting it off—by recognizing where it tries to speak—and putting on the new man through truth and renewal.

The old way of thinking is no longer your nature, but it can still show up as habit. That's why Paul gives us three clear movements:

1. Put Off the Old Self

The old self isn't who you are anymore—but its patterns may still show up. Paul says it's *"corrupted by deceitful desires."* That means the old self is built on lies—things you used to believe about God, about yourself, about how the world works. These lies formed reactions, coping strategies, and behaviors that made sense before—but no longer serve who you are now.

Putting off the old self doesn't mean fixing all your behavior. It means recognizing the lie behind the behavior.

For example:

* If fear is running your decisions, the lie might be *"I'm not safe."*

* If you lash out in anger, the lie might be *"I have to protect myself because no one else will."*

* If you constantly seek approval, the lie might be *"I'm only valuable when I perform well."*

To *"put off"* is to say:

"That's not who I am anymore. I may have believed that once, but it no longer defines me."

It's a moment of spiritual ownership. You're not pretending the lie doesn't exist—you're refusing to give it permission to lead your life.

2. Be Renewed in the Spirit of Your Mind

This is where the deep transformation happens—not just behavior change, but heart-level reprogramming. The *"spirit of your mind"* refers to the atmosphere of your thoughts—the tone, the assumptions, the quiet voice running underneath everything. Renewal here means you begin to think in alignment with truth—not by force, but by saturation.

Romans 12:2 puts it this way:

"Do not be conformed to this world, but be transformed by the renewing of your mind."

To be renewed means to reimagine your life through the lens of God's promises. It means letting grace reshape your inner world so that your outer world begins to change.

This is where Scripture meditation becomes essential. You're not just reading words—you're letting those words take root. You're giving the truth time to speak louder than the lie. This is where you plant the seed and water it with repetition, attention, and intention.

Practical ways to renew your mind:

* Speak first-person confessions from scripture daily

* Rehearse the truth out loud when the lie tries to resurface

* Visualize yourself walking in that truth, fully free

* Journal your real thoughts and invite the Spirit into them

* Memorize key verses that reinforce your identity in Christ

Over time, the truth doesn't just feel true—it becomes your normal.

3. Put On the New Self

This is where it gets beautiful. You don't just take something off—you put something better on. Paul says this new self is created after the likeness of God—not someday, but now. This is who you already are in Christ.

Putting on the new self is agreeing with that identity and walking in it—even before you feel like it's fully yours. It's not performance—it's alignment.

You begin to say:

* *"I am loved, even when I feel insecure."*
* *"I am righteous, even when I make mistakes."*
* *"I am whole, even while I'm still healing."*
* *"I am not trying to become new—I already am. I'm just learning to live like it."*

Putting on the new man means showing up as the real you—the one who is joined to Christ, filled with the Spirit, and empowered to live in righteousness and holiness.

This doesn't happen all at once. But every time you respond to life from this identity—rather than your past—you're practicing the new self. And over time, it gets easier. The new self becomes your default. And your old patterns lose their grip.

A Daily Exchange

Think of Ephesians 4:22–24 as your daily spiritual rhythm:

1. What lie is surfacing?

6. What does the Word say instead?

7. What does it look like to live from that truth today?

Here are some real-life examples of this daily exchange in practice:

* When you feel **rejected**, the lie may whisper, *"I'm not wanted."* But the truth from Ephesians 1:4 is clear: You are chosen by God before the foundation of the world. So in that moment, you can put off the pain of rejection and step into confidence and peace, knowing that you are handpicked by a loving Father.

* When you feel **anxious,** you may hear the lie, *"I'm not safe."* Yet Isaiah 41:10 tells you, *"Fear not, for I am with you."* So you put off anxiety and put on boldness and trust, walking through your day with the assurance that God Himself is with you, upholding you with His righteous right hand.

* When **condemnation** creeps in, the lie may sound like, *"I'm not enough."* But 2 Corinthians 5:21 declares that you are the righteousness of God in Christ Jesus. You put off that condemning voice and put on acceptance and freedom—standing tall in your full forgiveness and right standing before God.

* When you feel **insecure**, the lie may accuse, *"I'm too broken."* But Colossians 2:10 proclaims that you are complete in Him. So instead of retreating into shame, you put on strength and value, declaring that you lack nothing in Christ.

Each time you make that exchange—lie for truth, old for new—you're not just coping. You're training your heart and mind to walk in your new identity. Over time, these truths become instinctive, and the old self loses its voice.

This is the rhythm of renewal. And it's available to you, every single day. Repeat this as often as needed. It's not just information—it's transformation.

Reflection

* What old thoughts or behaviors still try to speak in my life?

* Have I been more focused on stopping sin, or putting on the truth?

* What truth do I need to speak to my heart today?

* What does it look like to live like the new person I already am?

First-Person Confession

I am not the person I used to be.

My old self is no longer in charge.

I put off the lies and the wounds they carried.

I am renewed in my mind by the Spirit of God.

I put on the new self—righteous, holy, and secure in Christ.

I walk in newness today, because He has made me new.

Prayer

Father, thank You for not just forgiving me, but recreating me.

Thank You for giving me a new self—born of Your Spirit, filled with Your power.

I put off the lies that have followed me. I put off the habits that no longer belong.

And I step into truth. I put on what You say is already mine.

Holy Spirit, renew my mind today.

Let truth run deeper than the old patterns.

Let grace strengthen me in every moment I feel weak.

I choose to live like the new person You've made me.

Thank You for never giving up on my transformation.

You're walking with me. And I'm not turning back.

In Jesus' name,
amen.

CHAPTER 13:
EXAMPLE WALKTHROUGHS

From reaction to renewal—real moments of putting off and putting on.

Sometimes the best way to learn how to live out spiritual truth is to see what it looks like in real life. This chapter is a practical look at how to apply Ephesians 4:22–24 in the everyday, messy, emotional moments when old lies resurface—and what it means to respond with truth.

These are not just stories. They're invitations. Use them to help identify your own patterns and start forming your own rhythm of renewal.

Walkthrough 1: Rejection and Belonging

The Moment:
You just finished speaking at a gathering of people you admire, but afterward, no one really acknowledged you. They complimented others but seemed to overlook you. A familiar ache hits: *"See? I'm invisible. I don't belong."*

The Lie:
"I'm not valuable. I don't belong unless others affirm me."

The Emotional Response:
You want to withdraw, shut down, and replay the moment to figure out what you did wrong. Your heart feels heavy, and your thoughts spiral into comparison and self-criticism.

Putting Off:
You pause and say, *"This feeling of rejection is real, but it's not the truth. I'm not going to let the voice of rejection define me anymore."*

Renewing the Mind:
You open to Ephesians 1:5 — *"He predestined us for adoption to sonship through Jesus Christ, in accordance with His pleasure and will."*

You sit with it and ask yourself:

* Do I believe God wanted me in His family?

* What does it mean that He chose me with joy?

Putting On:

You speak out loud:

"I am not rejected. I am adopted. I belong in God's family. His delight in me doesn't depend on applause. I am seen and chosen."

You walk back into the room—not looking for validation, but resting in identity.

Walkthrough 2: Fear and Trust

The Moment:

You get an unexpected bill in the mail. It's more than you can afford. Anxiety rises, and your chest tightens. You've been here before, and it always feels like drowning.

The Lie:

"I'm on my own. No one is going to take care of me."

The Emotional Response:

You feel panic, shame, and dread. Your mind rushes to worst-case scenarios. You begin rehearsing how you'll explain your failure.

Putting Off:
You breathe deeply and name the fear: *"This anxiety is trying to lie to me. I'm not abandoned. I'm not without help."*

Renewing the Mind:
You meditate on Philippians 4:19 – *"My God shall supply all your needs according to His riches in glory by Christ Jesus."*

You ask:
* Is my heart convinced He is my Provider?
* Can I let go of trying to figure this out in my strength?

Putting On:
You declare:

"God is my source. He is not surprised. He is faithful. I choose to trust Him right now."

Even if the anxiety doesn't fully lift, you've made a faith-based decision. That's victory.

Walkthrough 3: Shame and Righteousness

The Moment:
You snapped at your spouse in frustration. Now guilt and self-loathing sink in. *"Why can't I get this right? I should know better."*

The Lie:
"I'll never change. I'm a disappointment to God."

The Emotional Response:
You want to avoid prayer. You feel like you have to work your way back into God's good graces. There's distance in your heart.

Putting Off:
You say to yourself, *"Shame is not my teacher, and guilt is not my path to change. This mistake doesn't define me."*

Renewing the Mind:
You go to 2 Corinthians 5:21 – *"God made Him who knew no sin to be sin for us, so that in Him we might become the righteousness of God."*

You reflect:
* Do I believe that God sees me through the righteousness of Christ—even in this moment?
* Am I willing to come boldly, even when I feel low?

Putting On:
You whisper:

"I am still the righteousness of God in Christ. My behavior doesn't cancel my identity. Thank You, Jesus, for your mercy. I receive it right now."

Then you go and apologize—not as a failure trying to earn worth, but as a son or daughter walking in truth.

Walkthrough 4: Insecurity and Identity

The Moment:
You scroll social media and see a friend succeeding in an area where you feel behind—maybe marriage, parenting, ministry, or career. Suddenly you feel small, unseen, and stuck.

The Lie:
"I'm not enough. I'm falling behind. I'm not as valuable as they are."

The Emotional Response:
Jealousy flares up. You try to dismiss it, but it stings. You start to withdraw emotionally or hustle to prove something.

Putting Off:
You acknowledge, *"Comparison is a thief, and it doesn't speak for God. My value isn't up for debate."*

Renewing the Mind:
You turn to Colossians 2:10 – *"And in Him you have been made complete..."*

You ask:

* Do I believe I lack nothing in Christ?

* What am I trying to prove, and to whom?

Putting On:

You speak:

"I am complete in Christ. I have nothing to prove. I celebrate others because I'm secure in Him. I am already enough."

And with that, peace returns. You don't have to hide or strive. You're free to be fully you.

Final Thoughts

Each of these examples highlights the same process:

* Recognize the lie

* Replace it with truth

* Respond from your new identity

You will have moments where emotions rise first, where pain tries to talk louder than promise. But now you have tools. You have language. You have a Spirit-led process for transformation.

You're not fixing yourself. You're aligning with who God already made you to be.

Let your heart get used to that new normal. Practice it daily. You're not pretending—you're participating in the truth.

Reflection

* What are some recent moments when I reacted emotionally before remembering the truth?
* Can I identify the core lie underneath those reactions?
* What specific scriptures can I begin using to renew my mind in those areas?
* Am I willing to practice the exchange of truth for lies—even when I don't feel like it?
* Which of today's walkthroughs felt most like my own story?

First-Person Confession

I am not defined by my emotions or my past.

I am a new creation in Christ, and I choose to live from that identity.

When lies rise up, I replace them with God's truth.

I am learning to put off the old and put on the new—every single day.

This is my new rhythm, and grace is helping me grow.

CHOSEN AND LOVED

Prayer

Father, thank You for giving me a new way to live. You didn't just forgive me—you made me new. I don't have to live stuck in old thoughts or familiar patterns. You've given me truth, You've given me grace, and You've given me the Holy Spirit to walk with me.

Teach me to recognize lies quickly and respond with Your Word. Give me the wisdom to see what's happening in my heart, and the courage to make the exchange. Thank You for being patient with me and empowering me to grow.

This isn't about perfection—it's about transformation. And I say yes to that process. I trust You to finish what You started.

In Jesus' name,
Amen.

PART 6:
INTIMACY WITH GOD WHEN YOU'VE BEEN HURT

CHOSEN AND LOVED

Letting love draw you close again.

We were created for closeness with God. Not just obedience. Not just service. Closeness. Relationship. Intimacy.

But for many of us, that's the hardest part of the Christian life—not because God isn't willing, but because we've been wounded by people. We've been rejected, overlooked, betrayed, abandoned. And when that happens, it becomes difficult to trust—even with God.

Intimacy with Him can feel risky when closeness with others has been painful. Our hearts put up walls. We hide behind spiritual performance or theological correctness. We pray but keep Him at a safe distance. We serve but secretly wonder if He's disappointed. We say we believe—but avoid the tenderness of His gaze.

This part of the journey is about healing that distance.

It's about learning to let the love of God go deeper than the pain. To see that Jesus didn't just die for your sin—He died for your shame. He took your rejection. He bore your wounds. Not just so you could be saved, but so you could be close.

Isaiah 53 says He was *"despised and rejected by men... a man of sorrows and acquainted with grief."* He knows what it's like to be hurt. He knows what it's like to be misunderstood. He knows what it's like to love and be betrayed.

That's why He's safe.

In this section, we'll walk slowly through the process of letting love close the distance. You'll learn how to approach God not as a judge, but as a Father. Not with fear, but with boldness. You'll discover how to sit with Him even when you feel messy. And you'll find that He never flinches at your pain.

He wants you. Not the cleaned-up version of you. Just you. As you are. Right now.

This is where deep healing begins—face to face with the One who loves you most.

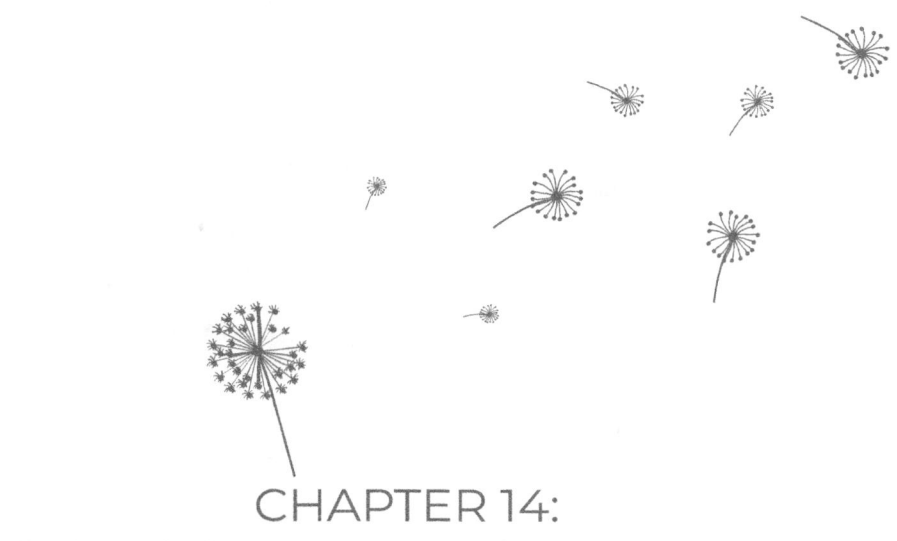

CHAPTER 14:
GOD IS SAFE BUT PAIN MAKES HIM FEEL FAR

Intimacy with God is one of the most beautiful gifts of the gospel. But for many, it's also the most intimidating. Not because God is distant—but because when pain is present, and we associate it with God's will, we push Him away in our hearts and minds..

When you've been hurt, especially by someone who should have loved you, closeness can feel dangerous. Even when you love God, your heart may instinctively keep Him at arm's length. You might fear what He'll say—or what He'll expect. And deep down, you may worry that if He really sees all of you, even He might turn away.

But the gospel tells a different story. It doesn't begin with your perfection—it begins with His pursuit. He didn't wait for you to be ready before coming close. While you were still broken, still guarded, still unsure—Jesus came. Not to demand something from you, but to give Himself for you.

The beginning of intimacy is not found in how much you can give to God—it starts when you see how much He gave for you.

The Cross Is Where Intimacy Begins

To understand the safety of God's love, we must look to the cross. The cross is not just about atonement—it's about invitation. It is where God shattered every barrier that stood between you and Him. Jesus didn't just die for your sin—He died for your shame. He carried your rejection, your abandonment, your betrayal.

Isaiah 53 tells us He was *"despised and rejected by men... a man of sorrows and acquainted with grief."* Jesus is not unfamiliar with your pain. He has felt it. He stepped into the human experience so He could walk beside you in yours—not with judgment, but with empathy.

You may have experienced deep wounds at the hands of others—parents who ignored you, friends who betrayed you, relationships that left you feeling worthless. But when you look at Jesus, arms stretched out, bearing every ounce of pain the world could throw at Him, you see something greater: a Savior who entered into rejection so you could be accepted forever.

This is where trust begins to grow. If Jesus went that far to bring you close, could you dare to believe that He's not backing away now?

Pain Builds Walls—but Love Waits on the Other Side

When you've been wounded, the soul learns to protect itself. Your brain may form defenses—automatic barriers built from fear, vows, and self-reliance. *"I'll never let anyone in again." "I'll handle it myself." "No one will ever get that close."*

Those walls may have felt necessary at the time. In moments of trauma or neglect, they helped you survive. But over time, they don't just keep danger out—they keep love out too. And that includes God's love.

But here's what's different about Him: He won't force

His way in. He knocks. He waits. He honors your timing, even when you're hesitant. Revelation 3:20 says, *"Behold, I stand at the door and knock."* He doesn't demand entrance. He invites you into relationship.

God doesn't break your walls with a battering ram—He melts them with love. His presence is not intrusive, but patient. He knows how it feels to be rejected, and He won't inflict the same pain on you. Instead, He gently waits for the smallest invitation. Even a whisper of willingness is enough for Him to enter.

When you say, *"God, I want to let You in, but I don't know how,"* that is enough. He'll take it from there.

God Is Not Like the Ones Who Hurt You

One of the hardest parts of healing is learning to separate God's love from the way people have treated you. Our nervous system doesn't distinguish easily between divine love and human failure. If we were neglected by a parent, manipulated by a partner, or hurt by church leaders, our heart tends to assume God is like them.

So we brace for disappointment. We try to earn His approval. We avoid His gaze. Deep down, we assume we have to prove ourselves to stay in His good graces.

But that is not the gospel.

Psalm 103 says that the Lord is like a compassionate father who remembers our frame, who knows we are dust. He is not waiting to catch you in failure. He's waiting to wrap you in mercy.

Jesus gave us the clearest picture of the Father's heart. In the story of the prodigal son, the son rehearses a speech—ready to grovel, to apologize, to beg his way back into the household. But the father runs to him, embraces him, clothes him in honor, and throws a feast. He doesn't even respond to the apology speech. He's too busy restoring the relationship.

That's how God responds to you.

You don't need to earn your way back into closeness with Him. You don't need to fix yourself first. He's already running toward you. You just have to let Him in.

It's Okay if Trust Feels Hard

Let's be honest—sitting still with God isn't always easy. Sometimes it feels awkward. Sometimes it surfaces old pain. Sometimes your body gets tense or your mind goes blank. That's not a sign of spiritual failure. It's a sign your heart is protecting something.

But God is not grading your performance. He's not asking for eloquent prayers or perfect posture. He's asking for honesty.

If the only thing you can say is, *"God, I don't know how to trust You,"* then say it. That is a beautiful and brave place to begin.

Psalm 34:18 says, *"The Lord is near to the brokenhearted."* Not just figuratively—He's emotionally present, right where you are. He's not startled by your pain. He's not disappointed in your doubts. He's near.

You don't have to force your heart to open all at once. Start with what you have. Whisper your fears. Sit with the tension. Let Him meet you in the places that still feel fragile.

He is not here to hurry you. He's here to hold you.

Practicing Presence—Without Pressure

Sometimes the simplest way to rebuild intimacy is by practicing being with God with no pressure, no performance, no need to *"do it right."*

Try this: find a quiet space. No music. No spiritual checklist. Just stillness. Take a deep breath. Let your body settle.

Picture Jesus—not far away, but near. Not scowling, but smiling. You don't have to imagine details. Just let your heart remember: He's here, and He's safe.

Say His name. *"Jesus."*

Let your thoughts wander if they need to. Let your emotions rise and fall without judgment. If sadness surfaces, let it come. If nothing comes at all, let that be okay too.

This is not about productivity. It's about presence.

And in that place—without pressure or performance—you'll begin to experience something sacred: the joy of simply being loved.

Reflection

* Have I ever feared that God would respond to me the way people have in the past?

* Where have I felt the need to perform or protect myself—even with God?

* What emotions rise when I try to sit in stillness with Him?

* Am I willing to let God come close, even if it feels uncomfortable at first?

* What would it look like to let myself be fully seen—and fully loved—by Him?

First-Person Confession

God, You are not like the ones who hurt me.

You are kind, patient, and safe.

I don't have to perform to be loved.

I don't have to protect myself from You.

I was made for closeness, and I say yes to that again.

Even when it's hard, I choose to trust Your love.

CHOSEN AND LOVED

Prayer

Father, I've kept You at a distance—not because I don't love You, but because I've been afraid. I've been hurt, and part of me still wonders if You'll hurt me too. But I see now—You're not like them. You're not distant or disappointed. You're the One who ran to me while I was still far off.

Jesus, thank You for entering into my pain, for carrying my rejection, and for proving Your love at the cross. You didn't just die for my sin—you died to bring me close. I want to trust You again. Help me lower my defenses. Help me sit with You, even when it feels vulnerable. Teach me that You're safe. Teach me that I'm safe in You.

I receive Your love again, right now. And I give You permission to come close.

Amen.

CHAPTER 15:
LEARNING TO RECEIVE LOVE AGAIN

Letting your heart be loved without earning or explaining.

It's one thing to say God loves you. It's another thing to feel it. To receive it. To let that love reach beneath the layers of pain, shame, defensiveness, and striving—and settle in your heart as truth.

For many of us, receiving love feels risky. It's not because we don't want love—it's because we've been shaped by rejection. When we've learned to survive through performance or self-protection, love can feel unfamiliar, even threatening. You may think, If I let myself feel this, what if it leaves again? What if it changes? What if I don't deserve it?

But the love of God is not like the love of man. It doesn't come and go. It isn't given based on performance or withdrawn when you fail. It's anchored in something far deeper: His nature.

1 John 4:16 says, *"We have come to know and to believe the love that God has for us. God is love."*

Notice the order: know and believe. You don't have to feel it immediately to receive it. Sometimes, receiving God's love is a choice you make before your emotions catch up. You choose to say, *"Even if I don't feel worthy, I believe You love me. And I'll open my heart to that love."*

That's where healing begins.

You Were Created to Be Loved

Before you were called to do anything for God, you were made to be loved by Him. You are not a tool in His hand—you are a child in His heart.

Ephesians 1:4–5 says that before the foundation of the

world, God chose you to be His, to be adopted into His family, to be holy and blameless in His sight in love. His entire plan for you is built on love.

Even your spiritual growth isn't about climbing a ladder of perfection—it's about being rooted and grounded in love (Ephesians 3:17). God knows that love is what changes you, sustains you, and anchors you.

The enemy would love for you to keep chasing approval, working harder to be accepted, trying to become lovable. But you already are. Right now. Not because of what you've done, but because of who He is.

Receiving His love is not selfish. It's not lazy. It's not emotional indulgence. It's the foundation of everything in the Christian life. Until you receive love, you'll struggle to trust Him, to rest in Him, to serve without striving.

Jesus said in John 15:9, *"As the Father has loved Me, I also have loved you; abide in My love."* Think about that. The way the Father loves Jesus—that's how Jesus loves you. There's no lack in that love. No insecurity. No rejection.

Abide in it. Settle down into it. Let it become your dwelling place.

Letting Go of Earning and Explaining

If you've ever felt the need to explain why you're worthy of love, you're not alone. Most of us learned early on that love had to be earned—by being helpful, by achieving, by hiding our flaws, or by never being a burden.

That survival strategy may have helped you cope, but it cannot help you receive grace.

Grace can't be earned. That's what makes it grace.

Romans 5:8 says, *"But God demonstrates His own love for us in this: While we were still sinners, Christ died for us."* He didn't wait until you had it all together. He chose you at your worst. And He hasn't changed His mind.

So here's the challenge: stop trying to convince God you're lovable. He's already convinced. And stop waiting to feel perfect before you open your heart. You won't get there by working harder. You'll get there by receiving more deeply.

When your thoughts tell you, *"I don't deserve this,"* you can answer, *"That's the point. It's not about deserving. It's about grace."*

You don't need to explain why God shouldn't love you. He already knows everything about you—and He chose to love you anyway.

How to Practice Receiving

Receiving love is not a one-time event. It's a practice—a posture you return to again and again.

Here's how you can begin:

1. Find a quiet space. Let yourself settle. Breathe deeply. Let go of performance.

2. Speak a simple truth aloud. Say something like: *"God, You love me. Right now. As I am."*

3. Notice your heart's response. Do you feel tension? Resistance? Shame? That's okay. Don't fight it—just notice it.

4. Stay present. Imagine Jesus standing before you, looking at you with compassion. Not analyzing. Not disappointed. Just loving.

5. Say yes. Even if your heart trembles, say: *"I receive Your love."* Say it again. And again. Until it begins to sink in.

You may cry. You may feel nothing. You may want to leave the moment altogether. That's okay. You're not failing. You're healing.

Each time you come back, that wall gets softer. That belief gets stronger. That love goes deeper.

Learning to receive love again is not about reaching an emotional high—it's about building a new foundation. One where God's love is your starting point, not a distant reward. One where you let go of the story that says you're too much or not enough. One where you begin to believe: I was made to be loved like this.

The love of God is not a concept to agree with—it's a reality to live from. And that reality starts with one small, powerful word: Yes.

Here are the **Reflection, Confession**, and **Prayer** sections for **Chapter 15: Learning to Receive Love Again:**

Reflection

* When I think about God loving me, what is my first emotional response?

* Do I feel the need to earn God's love, or explain why I'm worthy of it?

* Have I been avoiding stillness because it's hard to receive love without doing something?

* What would it feel like to truly rest in the love of God—no striving, no proving?

* Am I willing to practice receiving love even when I don't feel like I deserve it?

First-Person Confession

I was made to be loved by God.

I don't have to earn it. I don't have to explain myself.

I receive love because He freely gives it.

Even when it feels unfamiliar, I say yes to His affection.

His love is steady, safe, and healing—and it's mine.

CHOSEN AND LOVED

Prayer

Father, I want to receive Your love again—not just in my mind, but in my heart. You've always loved me, even when I didn't feel it, even when I pushed You away. Today, I stop trying to earn or explain. I stop hiding behind performance. I choose to open my heart.

Jesus, thank You for loving me the way the Father loves You. Thank You for proving that love by giving Yourself for me. Thank You that Your love isn't fragile or temporary—it's the anchor of my life.

Holy Spirit, help me stay in this place. Help me return to it again and again. Teach me to live rooted in love. And when old fears try to rise, remind me: I'm safe. I'm chosen. I'm deeply, permanently loved.

Amen.

PART 7:
LIVING WITH A RENEWED HEART

CHOSEN AND LOVED

Let your new identity shape the way you walk.

By now, you've seen that heart transformation isn't about behavior modification—it's about letting the truth of who God is rewrite what you believe about yourself, about Him, and about how you relate to the world.

You've seen how the Word discerns the heart, how false beliefs get exposed, and how intimacy with God heals the very places we once tried to hide. But the journey doesn't end there. The Christian life is not just a series of healing moments—it's a lifestyle of wholeness that flows from knowing who you are and whose you are.

This is what it means to live with a renewed heart.

A renewed heart doesn't mean you never struggle. It means you've learned how to stay anchored in your identity when the storms of life blow in. It means you know how to return to truth when lies try to resurface. It means you've built a habit of putting off the old, putting on the new, and walking daily in the love, power, and presence of God.

Romans 12:2 says, *"Do not be conformed to this world, but be transformed by the renewing of your mind..."* That transformation isn't a one-time event—it's a lifestyle. The more you believe what God believes about you, the more your inner world changes. And when your inner world is changed, your outer world begins to reflect it.

In this final section, we'll explore how to walk out this new identity in practical ways. We'll talk about daily rhythms that support your new heart. We'll look at what to do when you slip into old patterns. And we'll cast a vision for what it means to live free, whole, and fully loved—not just as a moment of breakthrough, but as your new normal.

You weren't just saved from something. You were saved for something.

You were given a new heart so you could live a new life—full of joy, peace, boldness, and deep connection with God.

Let's learn how to live from that place, every single day.

CHAPTER 16:
DAILY RHYTHMS OF HEART TRANSFORMATION

> *Forming a lifestyle that keeps your heart tender and your identity strong.*

Healing is not just a moment—it's a lifestyle. The transformation God begins in your heart through love, the Word, and renewed identity is meant to be nurtured, practiced, and lived. Just as trauma can become embedded in us through repetition and emotional intensity, truth and grace must be planted with intention and returned to regularly so they take deep root.

We don't stay free by accident. But we also don't stay free by striving. We stay free by rhythm—by creating patterns that keep us connected to the truth of who God is, who we are in Him, and how He's calling us to live.

That's what daily rhythms are for. These aren't religious duties—they're relational habits. They're how you return to your source again and again. Not to prove anything, but to stay soft, aligned, and whole.

Psalm 1 paints the picture:

"Blessed is the one… whose delight is in the law of the Lord, and who meditates on His law day and night. That person is like a tree planted by streams of water…" (Psalm 1:1–3)

Meditation. Stillness. Engagement. Return. These are the rhythms that keep your roots in the river.

Start With Stillness

Transformation begins in stillness. Before you read, journal, or even pray, let your heart come to rest. So much of our anxiety comes from trying to do for God without first being with Him.

Psalm 46:10 says, *"Be still, and know that I am God."* Stillness quiets the noise. It reminds your soul that He is near, that you are not in control—and that's okay. Begin your day, or any moment of reflection, by giving yourself space to simply be aware of Him.

Sit. Breathe. Acknowledge His presence. You don't have to feel anything spectacular. Let your soul know: God is here, and I am safe.

Meditate on the Word Like Food

Meditation is not just reading—it's receiving. Let the Word nourish your inner world the way food nourishes your body. Take one passage. Read it slowly. Speak it aloud. Picture it. Feel it.

Joshua 1:8 tells us to meditate *"day and night,"* because meditation moves the Word from your mind to your heart.

For example:

Take Romans 8:1 — *"There is therefore now no condemnation for those who are in Christ Jesus."*

Say it slowly. Then ask your heart:

* Do I feel condemned?

* Do I truly believe I'm free from guilt?

* What comes up when I hear this truth?

If you feel resistance, pause. Don't rush past it. This is where transformation begins—where the Word becomes a mirror. Remind yourself, This is the truth, no matter what I feel right now. And the truth will set me free.

Confess the Truth Out Loud

Your words help reinforce your beliefs. As you meditate, speak the truth over yourself—not as a performance, but as a declaration. Confession helps rewire your thoughts and emotions to align with your spirit.

Use personalized versions of scripture. For instance:

"I am in Christ, and there is no condemnation over my life."
"I am chosen, holy, and deeply loved."
"I have a new heart, and God is renewing my mind."

Over time, your inner world will begin to echo what you're speaking. This is not mindless repetition—it's intentional agreement with what God says is true.

Let Your Emotions Respond

As you sit with the Word and confess it, pay attention to your emotional response. Your feelings will often tell you where old beliefs still linger. But don't run from that discomfort—use it.

If tears rise, let them fall. If anger bubbles up, acknowledge it. If numbness surfaces, don't judge it. These reactions aren't disqualifiers—they're invitations. Invitations for God's truth to reach deeper, for grace to go where your pain lives.

Ask yourself:

* What am I really believing right now?
* What lie might be surfacing?
* What truth needs to be planted in its place?

Journal the Process

Writing out your discoveries helps you track what God is doing in you. Journaling isn't just a record—it's a conversation. Write what surfaced. Write the lie you noticed. Write the truth you're choosing to believe.

Even simple entries like:

* *"I read Psalm 34:18 today. It says God is close to the brokenhearted. But I didn't feel that. I remembered how abandoned I felt growing up. But I told myself—God is not like them. He doesn't leave. I'm going to keep meditating on that."*

This kind of journaling helps connect your mind, heart, and spirit. It honors your process. And over time, you'll look back and see how far you've come.

Return as Often as Needed

Don't turn rhythms into rigid rules. They're not about perfection—they're about return. The point is not how often or how long. It's that you come back. Every day if possible. Or every moment you feel off course.

God's love doesn't change when you miss a day. But your awareness of that love grows stronger when you return to Him regularly.

Even when your emotions are flat, even when you don't feel spiritual—show up. Keep planting. Truth is leaven. It will work its way through.

Final Thoughts

Your new heart is real. But your thoughts and emotions need time to adjust. The old patterns don't go away just because you had a revelation—they go away as you keep showing up with the truth.

These daily rhythms aren't about performance. They're about presence. They're how you let grace continue what it started. They're how you nourish the transformation that Jesus purchased for you.

A renewed heart becomes a renewed life—when you give it room to breathe, rest, and believe.

Reflection

* What part of my day could I consistently set aside to be with God—without pressure, just presence?

* When I read or speak God's Word, do I pause to let it affect my heart?

* How do I respond when I feel resistance or discomfort during meditation—do I shut down or stay open?

* What rhythms help me stay rooted in the truth of who I am?

* Where can I invite God into my routine more intentionally?

First-Person Confession

I was made to live from a renewed heart.

I don't have to earn God's presence—I get to enjoy it.

As I sit with the Word, it reshapes me.

As I speak truth, I grow stronger.

God meets me in my rhythms with healing, peace, and joy.

I return to Him daily—and He always welcomes me.

> **Prayer**
> Father, thank You for making my heart new. Thank You for inviting me into daily fellowship with You—not through pressure, but through grace. Help me find rhythms that feed my soul and renew my mind. Teach me to love Your Word, not as a duty, but as a place of connection and life.
> Holy Spirit, guide me in stillness. Help me be honest as I read, gentle with myself when old pain surfaces, and bold in speaking truth. Let every rhythm I build create more space for You.
> I trust that as I return again and again, Your love will continue to transform me.
> I belong in Your presence, and I choose to live from that place every day.
> Amen.

CHAPTER 17: STAYING ROOTED IN GRACE

When pressure rises, let grace be your ground.

Living with a renewed heart doesn't mean you'll never face old thoughts, emotions, or temptations. But it does mean you now have a new foundation—a new place to return to when life pulls at your peace.

That foundation is grace.

Grace is more than forgiveness. It's the empowering presence of God, working in you, helping you walk out who you truly are. Grace is God's kindness, strength, and patience toward you as you grow. And the more deeply rooted you are in grace, the less you'll be shaken when things get hard.

Galatians 5:1 says, *"It is for freedom that Christ has set us free. Stand firm, then, and do not let yourselves be burdened again by a yoke of slavery."*

Freedom is your new normal. But it requires choosing grace over performance, truth over condemnation, and love over fear—again and again.

Grace Is the Soil Where Growth Happens

Think of your heart like a garden. Grace is the rich soil where the seeds of truth take root. Without grace, we fall back into performance-based thinking—believing we have to earn transformation or prove our worth.

But in grace, there's space to grow.

Grace means:

* You can fail forward without shame.
* You can take time to heal without being rushed.
* You can be honest about your process without fear of rejection.

God's grace is not a license to stay stuck—it's the power to move forward without condemnation hanging over you.

Titus 2:11–12 says, *"For the grace of God has appeared, bringing salvation to all people. It teaches us to say 'No' to ungodliness and worldly passions, and to live self-controlled, upright and godly lives..."*

Grace teaches you. It doesn't punish—it coaches. It trains your heart to follow God's voice, not out of fear, but out of love and trust.

What to Do When You Slip

Renewing your mind and living from the heart is not a linear journey. You will have days when the old patterns resurface. That doesn't mean you're back at square one—it means you need grace.

On those days, stop and remind yourself:

"God's love hasn't changed. His Spirit hasn't left. My identity is still secure. I'm still new. I just forgot for a moment."

Romans 5:2 says that we have access by faith into this grace in which we now stand. Grace is your standing place. It's where you get up again—not through shame, but through mercy and truth.

If you feel triggered, reactive, or defeated—pause. Breathe. Remind yourself who you are. Speak the truth you've been planting. Go back to a verse you've meditated on. And let that truth reset your heart.

Even if the same lie comes up again, grace says, *"Let's deal with it again, with love and power."*

Don't Measure Progress by Emotion

Sometimes we expect that a renewed heart will always feel peaceful or joyful. But growth often feels quiet. You may not always *"feel"* different—but grace is still working. Just like leaven in dough, it spreads slowly, invisibly, until the whole heart is affected.

Philippians 1:6 gives you this promise:

"He who began a good work in you will carry it on to completion until the day of Christ Jesus."

You don't have to carry yourself. You just have to stay rooted in the One who is faithful to complete what He started.

Grace is patient. Grace is steady. Grace believes in you even when you struggle to believe in yourself.

Return to Grace—Again and Again

This is your rhythm now:
Not fear.
Not perfectionism.
Not self-effort.
But grace.

Grace that says:

* *"You're still chosen."*

* *"You're still my child."*

* *"Let's try again, together."*

Return to grace when your heart feels dry. Return to grace when you feel ashamed. Return to grace when you forget who you are.

You are not beyond God's reach. And your story is not stuck.

In grace, you are rooted—and in grace, you will grow.

Reflection

* When I mess up or feel triggered, what do I usually turn to—shame, hiding, or grace?

* Do I still believe deep down that I have to earn God's love or favor?

* What would change if I truly believed that grace is both my starting point and my daily ground?

* How do I respond to slow growth—do I celebrate progress or feel discouraged?

* Where do I need to return to grace today?

First-Person Confession

I am rooted in grace.

God's love for me never changes—even when I feel weak.

I don't have to earn what Jesus already paid for.

When I fall, grace lifts me up.

When I forget, grace reminds me.

When I'm tired, grace carries me.

I am growing every day, because grace is alive in me.

Prayer

Father, thank You for Your unwavering love. Thank You that grace isn't just for when I get it right—it's for every part of my journey. When I fall short, You don't push me away. You draw me back with kindness. Help me stay grounded in that grace, no matter what I face.

Holy Spirit, remind me that growth takes time, and I don't need to rush. Let me feel safe with You, even when old patterns resurface. Teach me to live from grace—to speak truth when I forget, to rise again when I fall, and to rejoice in progress, no matter how small.

I rest in what Jesus has done. I trust that You are completing what You began in me.

Amen.

CHAPTER 18:
TRANSFORMATION THAT LASTS

> *The truth planted in your heart is becoming your way of life.*

By now, you've journeyed through healing, exposure, belief, and renewal. You've learned how trauma writes lies on the heart—and how truth can rewrite them. You've seen how intimacy with God restores your sense of safety and identity. And you've experienced the power of the Word to discern, divide, and transform. Now it's time to settle into the life this renewal was always meant to produce.

Real transformation doesn't fade.

It doesn't wear off like emotion.
It deepens with time, like roots reaching further into the soil of God's love.

But it's not automatic.
The truth that brings lasting change is the truth you keep walking in.

Transformation Is Not a Moment—It's a New Way of Living

Many people look for breakthrough experiences—powerful encounters or emotional highs. And while God can absolutely move that way, most of the transformation that sticks happens quietly, gradually, and consistently.

The parable of the sower (Mark 4) shows us that the Word is seed. Some seed gets choked. Some gets stolen. But when it's planted in good soil—an honest, receptive heart—it produces fruit with endurance.

You've prepared your heart.

You've planted the Word.

Now your job is to keep the soil healthy—and keep

tending the garden.

Transformation lasts when:

* You protect the truth from being choked by distractions.

* You revisit and speak the truth even when you feel nothing.

* You turn to grace when you stumble, instead of shame.

* You walk with God, not just during *"quiet times,"* but in your thoughts, relationships, and everyday choices.

You Were Made to Bear Fruit

Jesus said in John 15:8, *"This is to my Father's glory, that you bear much fruit, showing yourselves to be my disciples."*

This isn't about performance—it's about becoming.
You were made to live a life that reflects God's love, grace, and truth.
A life where peace is normal.
A life where joy runs deeper than circumstances.
A life where intimacy with God is natural and constant.
A life that helps others heal just by being near you.
And it's all possible—because He made you new.

Let the Word Keep Shaping You

You've seen how the Word discerns and reveals. But it also builds and strengthens. It feeds your heart daily. And every time you speak it, believe it, or return to it—it does its work again.

Hebrews 10:14 says, *"By one sacrifice he has made perfect forever those who are being made holy."* That's the balance of the new life: you're already made perfect in spirit, and you're still being shaped in your soul.

So keep speaking the Word, even when it feels repetitive.

Keep choosing the truth, even when emotions disagree.

Keep receiving grace, even when the enemy tries to accuse.

This is how transformation becomes permanent.

You Are Now a Living Testimony

The same love that healed you will heal others.

The same Word that discerned your heart will set others free.

The same Jesus who walked you through shame, fear, and rejection is ready to lead others—through you.

You are not only chosen. You are **sent.**

You are not only healed. You are a **healer.**

You are not only whole. You are **a reflection of God's wholeness** to the world.

What God began in you is just the beginning. You are a living testimony.

So live boldly. Live loved.

Live like someone who is, without a doubt, chosen by God.

Reflection

* Where have I already seen real, lasting transformation take root in me?

* What truth has become more natural to believe now than it was before?

* How can I guard the Word God has planted in me as I move forward?

* What fruit do I want my life to bear in the next season?

Confession

I am not the same as I was.

The Word has changed me. The truth has healed me.

God has planted His life in me, and it's bearing fruit.

I walk with Him. I stay rooted in grace.

I will keep growing, keep becoming, and keep showing the world what it looks like to be loved.

> **Prayer**
> Father, thank You for walking me through this journey.
> Thank You for not just healing the wounds—but giving me a new heart, a new identity, and a new future. I believe I am transformed—and I will continue to be transformed by Your Spirit and truth.
> Jesus, thank You for finishing the work. Thank You for bearing every lie, every sin, every rejection—and giving me Your victory in return.
> Holy Spirit, stay close. Guide my rhythms. Speak to my heart. Empower my days. Let my life be a reflection of Your love and a testimony of what it means to live renewed.
> I am Yours. Fully. Freely. Forever.
> Amen.

CONCLUSION:

You're Becoming Whole

You've come a long way.

You've done something brave—something most people never do. You looked inward. You invited the Holy Spirit into the vulnerable places of your heart. You listened to the Word, not just as a religious practice, but as a mirror of your true identity. And maybe for the first time, you began to see yourself the way God sees you: chosen, loved, worthy, and whole in Christ.

That's not small. That's miraculous.

But this isn't the end of the journey—it's the beginning of a new way of living. A life rooted in truth. A life led by the Spirit. A life shaped not by rejection or pain, but by the unshakable love of God.

As you continue, remember this: healing is a process. It takes time. The wounds that formed in childhood, through betrayal, neglect, or trauma, won't always disappear in a moment. But every time you speak truth, every time you meditate on God's promises, every time you pause to receive love where pain used to reign—you are being transformed.

Let that transformation go deep. Let it be slow if it needs to be. You don't need to rush to get to some perfect version of yourself. Jesus already made you righteous. You're not striving to be accepted—you're learning to live as one who already is.

And while this book has given you tools, exercises, and daily rhythms to help you renew your mind and heart, **don't become dogmatic.** These tools are here to serve your healing, not control your process. If one practice or exercise resonates deeply with you, lean into it. If another feels heavy or unhelpful in a certain season, let it go without guilt. The Holy Spirit is your guide. Grace will lead you.

You may need to come back to these truths again and again. That's okay. In fact, it's good. Just like the earth receives rain season after season, your heart will continue to soften and bloom as you let God's truth water it again and again.

So stay tender.
Stay curious.
Stay open to love.

Let the Word keep planting truth in you.
Let God's love be the safety that your heart never had.

Let your identity in Christ become the lens through which you see everything else.

You are not the rejected one.
You are not the forgotten one.
You are not the broken one.

You are the one He came for.
You are chosen. You are loved.
And you are becoming whole.

Not someday. Not when you're stronger.
But **now**—as you believe, and receive, and rest in His love.

This is your new beginning. And grace will carry you the whole way.

ABOUT THE AUTHOR

Clint Byars (www.clintbyars.com) is the lead pastor of Forward Church in Sharpsburg, Georgia (www.forward.church). With a message rooted in the finished work of Jesus and the believer's identity in Christ, Clint's passion is to help people experience lasting transformation by renewing the mind and persuading the heart with truth.

His teaching blends biblical theology with practical tools for spiritual growth, often integrating insights from neuroscience, quantum physics, and emotional healing. Clint's approach is both revelatory and grounded—anchored in Scripture, yet boldly exploring how God's Word brings life to every part of our being.

Through books, sermons, and ministry training, Clint empowers believers to live from the Spirit, walk in the fullness of grace, and participate in God's kingdom with joy and purpose. He and his wife Sara lead Forward Church together, raising up a community of believers who are rooted in love, grounded in grace, and equipped to impact the world.

You can find more teachings, devotionals, and resources from Clint at clintbyars.com or forward.church. Courses are also available at www.forwardschooloftransformation.

com.

Men, visit www.strongandgodlymen.com for a course to Equip you to Build and Lead.

More Books by Clint Byars

Devil Walk: A True Story of Drugs, Demonic Possession, and Deliverance

Who Do You Love?: Discover How to Live from Purpose and Fulfill Your Call

Paul's Prophetic Lens: Paul's Journey to Faith-Righteousness through the Law and Prophets

Seeds of Prosperity: A Workbook for Planting God's Financial Wisdom in Your Heart

God Says Yes to Over 3000 Promises

In Christ: A Meditation Devotional In Your New Creation Identity In Christ

Gifts of the Spirit Training Manual

All available here: https://www.clintbyars.com/books

www.ingramcontent.com/pod-product-compliance
Lightning Source LLC
Chambersburg PA
CBHW051830090426
42736CB00011B/1729